Guess the Firstborn

I'll give you a pair of names, and you pick the firstborn in each pair.

1. Jennifer Aniston or Courtney Cox Arquette
2. Harrison Ford or Martin Short
3. Ulysses S. Grant or Robert E. Lee
4. Ellen DeGeneres or Oprah Winfrey
5. Bill Cosby or Chevy Chase

If you picked Aniston, Ford, Grant, Winfrey, and Cosby, you're right. (Ulysses S. Grant not only helped win the Civil War, but he was the only general ever to get his likeness on a fifty-dollar bill.)

Try these next five and see how you do:

1. Bill Clinton or Ronald Reagan
2. Steve Martin or Jay Leno
3. Jacqueline Kennedy or Whoopi Goldberg
4. Martin Luther King Jr. or Jim Carrey
5. Matthew Perry or Arnold Schwarzenegger

If you picked Clinton, Martin, Kennedy, King, and Perry, you're right. See how good at this you are?

"But wait right there, Dr. Leman," you're saying. "Why are you calling Steve Martin a firstborn? I happen to know he's the youngest kid in his family. And there's no way Martin Luther King Jr. is a firstborn. He had an older sister."

Ah, but they are firstborns. And you might be too, even if you weren't the first child born in your family. For why, read on.

Born
to Win

Keeping Your Firstborn Edge
without Losing Your Balance

Dr. Kevin Leman

Revell
a division of Baker Publishing Group
Grand Rapids, Michigan

Published by Revell
a division of Baker Publishing Group
P.O. Box 6287, Grand Rapids, MI 49516-6287
www.revellbooks.com

Paperback edition published 2009

Previously published under the title *The Firstborn Advantage*

Printed in the United States of America

Library of Congress Cataloging-in-Publication Data
Leman, Kevin.
    Born to Win : keeping your firstborn edge without losing your balance / Kevin Leman.
        p.   cm.
    Includes bibliographical references.
    ISBN 978-0-8007-3262-2 (pbk.)
    1. Birth order. 2. First-born children—Psychology. I. Title.
BF723.B5L4633 2009
155.9'24—dc22   2009018956

To protect the privacy of those who have shared their stories with the author, some details and names have been changed.

Your birth was our wonderful, precious gift from God. As new, excited parents, we made all the mistakes. Yes, we admit we practiced on you. You, our firstborn, were our guinea pig. But what a great privilege it has been for us to be your dad and mom throughout all these years. You're an achiever with the priceless qualities of grace, compassion, and wisdom. We couldn't be more proud of you.

Contents

Contents

Acknowledgments

To Ramona Tucker: Thank you for your dedication and hard work in making this book all it could be. I appreciate so much the opportunity to work with you. I love the fact that you shoot it to me straight and that you are a woman of integrity.

Grateful thanks also to Laura Carter, founder of the First Born Girls Social Club (www.firstborngirls.com), for her invaluable insight on what it means to be a firstborn woman; and to Bob Shaff, founder and president of Customers for Life Consulting (www.cflconsulting.com), for his "14 Actions Your Company Can Take to Earn Customer Loyalty."

Introduction

Will the Firstborn Please Stand Up?

Just who are the firstborns?

How many firstborns did you peg in the "Guess the First-born" quiz? Total up the ones you got right. Okay, got your answer?

I'd bet my wife and a couple of my five children on the fact that you were able to pick out all ten, or at least nine out of ten.

Now how did that happen? What is it about these firstborns that stand out from the rest? And why?

You don't have to have a PhD in psychology to figure out who the firstborns in the world are. Firstborns are the natural movers and shakers. They're the leaders. They can accomplish just about anything.

Think of the governor of your state, the US senators, the mayor of your town, the president of your school board, the head of the company you work for. Chances are, they're all firstborn children.

If you're reading this book on an airplane or a commuter train, chances are high that the person across from you doing a crossword puzzle or Sudoku book is a firstborn. If you're an adventurous sort, why don't you ask the stranger, "Do you happen to be a firstborn?" Who knows? You might end up with a lively conversation on your hands.

Certain professions also seem to attract firstborns. For example, in my hometown of Tucson, Arizona, there is a group of twelve anesthesiologists. Nine of them just happen to be firstborns, and the other three are only children—the only children in a family—which are basically first cousins emotionally to firstborns. Is this happenstance, do you think? Or is there something about firstborns that attracts them to the precision required for such a career?

Neil Armstrong, the first man to walk on the moon, was a firstborn (the eldest of three children). All of the Mercury Seven astronauts were firstborns. In fact, of the first twenty-three astronauts in outer space, twenty-one were firstborns. The other two were only children. There wasn't a middle or youngest child in sight.

The majority of the US presidents have been firstborns.[1] Frank Sulloway, a brilliant MIT researcher who wrote *Born to Rebel: Birth Order Family Dynamics and Creative Lives*, claims that firstborns tend to be more conscientious, more conservative, more responsible, more achievement oriented, and more organized than laterborns, who tend to be more open-minded and willing to take risks and explode cherished ideas and theories. Firstborns stuck with the status quo and were very assertive about it. No wonder firstborns are in so many of the top positions of leadership.[2]

Take, for instance, the 2008 US presidential election. The final three contenders for the biggest job in the world were an only child (Barack Obama—more later on why he's considered an only child), a firstborn daughter (Hillary Clinton), and a firstborn son (John McCain).

There is truly something unique about firstborns, the leaders of the pack. You may be one of them. Or you may be one of them and not know it. (More on that in this book too.) But how did they—and you—get to be that way?

> Firstborns are the natural movers and shakers of the world. They're the leaders. They can accomplish just about anything.

Take a look at your own family—your brothers and sisters. Isn't it true that the firstborn and secondborn are day-and-night different? And if you're a parent today, isn't it true that if your firstborn travels east, your secondborn will travel west? These differences can be explained by birth order.

If you're reading this book, chances are it's because you're a firstborn, or you know (and are driven crazy by) a firstborn. Firstborns can take the world by storm—and accomplish more than you think is humanly possible, because they are exacting and precise.

But out of balance they become driven, overly perfectionistic, and critical-eyed. Just imagine a group of firstborns getting together to wallpaper your kitchen. Within thirty minutes there would be blood on the floor, since everyone would want to be in charge. That's why baby-of-the-family folks like me are so needed. Without the balance of middle-borns and lastborns, firstborns can become too intense on completing the task "the right way" (translation: "their way") and lose the relationship. Then they make their own and others' lives miserable.

For instance, take Mrs. Marcourt, the den mother of my Cub pack when I was young. I was actually asked to leave the Cub Scouts because she didn't appreciate my baby-of-the-family antics. She had little tolerance for them. What had happened to bring this about? Well, I ask you, if a bunch of boys were coming over and you wanted to serve them chocolate chip cookies, would you place those cookies on your grandmother's precious china serving dish?

I destroyed that dish in one fell swoop. All I was doing was diving for the first chocolate chip cookie. What was wrong with that?

Mrs. Marcourt had a lot to say to me about what was wrong with that. And she also told my mother in no uncertain terms what was wrong with that. I didn't return to Cub Scouts.

You see, Mrs. Marcourt was a firstborn. She was determined to do things right, and only she knew what the right way was. (The same goes for my firstborn wife, who starts preparing for a meal on Thursday when company isn't coming until Saturday.)

"But, Dr. Leman," you're saying, "I'm not the firstborn in my family, but I sure act like it. And my older sister, the first child born in our family, doesn't act like a firstborn at all. Why is that?"

Why would I call a guy like Steve Martin, who is the youngest kid in his family, a firstborn? And why would I call Martin Luther King Jr., who has an older sister, a firstborn? Because you can be number eight in a family of nine, like my mother, and still be a firstborn. You can be number five in a family and still have a firstborn personality. You can have an older sibling, like Martin Luther King Jr., and still have a firstborn personality.

"Uh, Dr. Leman," you're saying, as you roll your eyes, "you better get some help with math. Things aren't adding up very well for you. How can you be a firstborn if you're not born first? That makes absolutely no sense."

Ah, but it makes perfect sense. I'll show you why in this book. There are a lot of myths floating around about this whole birth order business, and I'm determined to debunk them. All the years of research and study behind the scientific theory of birth order don't really mean much until the principles learned are actually *applied* to people like you— to help you understand yourself and improve your life. And that's what I love doing best.

So we'll take a look at birth order in the family. Although it's impossible to pigeonhole everyone into airtight compartments, at the same time it's true that most firstborns tend to display certain characteristics, as do most middleborns and lastborns (or "babies," as I like to call them). Your ordinal position—the order in which you were born in the family—is very important. It has everything to do not only with your place in the family but with how you live your entire life.

But there are other critical variables that greatly influence your birth order as well. As we talk about these, chances are you'll have an "Aha!" regarding your birth family, your spouse, or one or more of your children. "Now I know why my sister drives me so crazy," you'll say. Or, "Now I know why my husband acts the way he does." Or, "Oh, I get it. My son is actually a firstborn. Now that makes sense."

We'll identify both successes and weaknesses of the first-born personality. We'll figure out why firstborns are the way they are. Is it because they got first pick on the genetic material? Is it because of the way they were reared? Or is it a combination of factors?

Once you understand how your ordinal and functional birth order affects your personality, you'll be able to see your own strengths and weaknesses. You'll realize why you make certain choices, whether wise or poor, in life. And then you can begin to strengthen yourself, to improve on the areas in which you're weak, and to make the strong parts of your personality even stronger.

"Balance is a crucial issue for a firstborn," says Laura Carter, founder of the First Born Girls Social Club. "Firstborns need *permission* to be able to relax. We struggle commonly with time management, stress management, and prioritizing because we tend to take on a lot . . . in fact, too much."[3]

Does that sound like you, firstborn? We'll talk about how important balance is particularly to firstborns, and I'll give you a peek into the heads of those in the First Born Girls Social Club. My guess is that, if you're a firstborn woman, you'll find—as the misunderstood Anne did in *Anne of Green Gables*—"a bosom buddy" in those women. (And hey, maybe someday someone will think of starting a First Born Guys Social Club. But my guess is that no one would show up since "being relational" is not usually at the forefront of a firstborn male's mind.)

We'll also talk about why firstborns in particular have a heightened sensitivity and response to "the critical eye." If there's anything that firstborns struggle with, it's flaw picking.

Did you have a critical-eyed parent? (It only takes one to influence you for a lifetime. If you had two critical-eyed parents, you *really* need to read chapter 6.) Do you struggle with your own perfectionism as a result? Do you tend to pick at others' flaws? This one single variable—the critical eye—is so critical to the success or failure of a firstborn that I've devoted an entire chapter to it.

When faced with a critical-eyed parent, firstborns tend to become either pleasers (doing everyone else's bidding, with no thought to themselves) or controllers ("I'm in charge, and it's got to be my way—it's the only right way"). But you don't have to live daily with that kind of stress—or the power struggle. I'll show you how to sidestep it.

Once you understand your firstborn personality—why you are the way you are and what variables contributed to who you are—you can move forward in confidence to use your firstborn skills to your best advantage at home, at school, at work, and in your relationships.

Why do you tend to marry someone of a different birth order than you, but your friends tend to be of the same birth order? How can you motivate your children to do well in school—without frustrating them or exhausting yourself with homework battles? Why are you the only one who is annoyed by the smells emanating from the work refrigerator? How can you win at business all the time? I'll reveal those secrets in upcoming chapters.

As a firstborn, you spend so much time fulfilling others' expectations. But what about your own dreams? What do you want to do and be? How can those firstborn qualities help you?

That's what *Born to Win* is all about.

One last thing before you turn the page. Want to take another shot at guessing the firstborn? Then try these pairs:

1. Matt Damon or Ben Affleck
2. Florence Henderson (*Brady Brunch* mom) or Martha Stewart
3. Reese Witherspoon or Sheryl Crow
4. Ben Stiller or Billy Crystal
5. Angelina Jolie or Brad Pitt

See page 57 for the answers.

1

What's This Birth Order Business About Anyway?

It has everything to do with your place in the family—
and your entire life.

The instant the woman next to me on the plane pulled out her Sudoku book, I knew what birth order she was. I couldn't help myself.

I leaned over and asked her, "You're a firstborn daughter, aren't you?"

She stared at me. "Why did you assume I'm a firstborn daughter?"

I smiled. "I'll tell you, if you'll confirm it."

"Yes, I'm a firstborn daughter."

And so I told her about herself, all based on her birth order.

Her jaw dropped. "You just described who I am. How did you know that?"

I smiled again. "It's all in your birth order." I paused. "Do you have a younger sister?"

She nodded.

"Mind if I describe her for you and see how I do?"

She nodded again.

So I described the baby of the family: "The life of the party, social butterfly, doesn't get as good of grades, well liked by peers, helpless as a clam, great at getting her firstborn sister— you—in trouble, outgoing, never met a stranger, etc."

By now the woman's jaw had dropped again. "This is the most fascinating conversation I've ever had."

It wasn't because I was a fascinating conversationalist. It's because the concept of birth order itself is so fascinating. After all, *everyone* has a birth order. And that birth order has everything to do with not only your place in the family but your entire life.

Birth Order in Motion

There's an exercise I enjoy doing as an icebreaker in school settings when teachers have an in-service day. It's so fun to watch the reactions. You may want to try it yourself in a group setting sometime.

After the teachers have filed into the room and settled in, I'll ask the participants to divide up according to birth order. All the firstborns and only children move their chairs into one corner, the middle children into another, and the last-borns into another. Then I ask them to stand up and arrange themselves in a circle.

Once they're in their circles, I do a bit of screening. It's not tough for anyone to figure out if they're born first in a family, so I concentrate on the middle and lastborn circles.

I ask the middles, "Are you more than five years younger than the same-sex child above you in the family?" If so, I weed those people out of the middle circle, because they're not true middle children.

I ask the babies, "Are you the only one of your sex in the family? Or are you five or more years younger than the same-sex child above you?" If so, I weed those people out of the baby circle, because they're not true babies. (More on this later.)

When I know I have true firstborn, middle, and lastborn groups, I walk around and place a piece of paper on the floor in the middle of each group. Once I've left the paper on the floor, I don't do anything else. The groups just stand there for a while, looking nervously at each other, wondering just what kind of speaker I am. When am I going to tell them what they're supposed to do?

But of course, I'm not going to tell them anything.

It's not usually too long before someone in the firstborn and only-children group takes the initiative and picks up the paper. Once in a great while someone in the group of middle children or even the lastborn group will pick up the paper first, but this happens about as often as it snows in my hometown of Tucson.

Usually the group of gregarious lastborns will be so involved in chitchat and getting to know each other that I can only assume they've completely forgotten the purpose of the seminar.

Here's what I'll have written on that paper:

Congratulations! You are the leader of this group. Please introduce yourself to the others in your group and then have each person do the same. As you talk together, make a list of the personality characteristics that you all seem to share. Be prepared to report back to the rest of the seminar participants with your "composite picture" of yourselves. Please start to work immediately.

Within a second the firstborns and only children are in high gear, talking like woodpeckers on a fir tree.

Then the middleborn children (good observers of life that they are) might happen to notice something going on. If they do, they get involved. They tentatively pick up the paper.

But the babies? Their circle looks more like a snaking river going through a canyon, wiggling all over the place. They are talking, giving each other high fives, and enjoying life—completely oblivious to the project twenty feet from them in the next group.

I'll wait for twenty minutes or so and then announce, "You have another five minutes to get your work completed."

At this point, the firstborns (and middleborns, if they're astute—this varies from group to group) already working on their list will begin working faster, whereas the babies (and sometimes the middleborns) will either look at me blankly, as if I'm totally out of my mind, or just ignore me and keep on with their small talk.

Naturally, when the time is up and I ask the different groups to make their reports, the firstborns and only children are always well prepared; the middleborns are, as usual, in the middle—sometimes prepared, sometimes not; and the embarrassed lastborns always try to explain, through their nervous laughter, that they didn't do anything because I never told them what they were supposed to be doing. They saw me put the piece of paper on the floor, but they figured I was going to tell them what it was all about.

That demonstration is birth order in motion. When people in the audience get it, they start to howl, for that little exercise illustrates clearly that firstborns are most generally the leaders—the ones who see what needs to be done, then plunge ahead and do it. The firstborns are out there on the cutting edge, daring to take risks (but still within the status quo, per research by birth order expert Frank Sulloway), while their younger brothers and sisters most often wait to be told what their role is supposed to be.

Taking the initiative is a natural tendency of firstborns, and it's a quality that often leads them to positions of leadership. So it's no wonder that, as I've said earlier, firstborns are prominent in leadership positions.

This innate leadership ability thus serves the firstborn well. But it can also drive her crazy. Why do I say that? Does a firstborn mind being a leader? No. She's not *really* bothered by the fact that no one else sees what has to be done until she points it out. From day one of her life, she's been used to that. What drives her absolutely crazy is the fact that even *after* she points to the problem and articulates what needs to be done, almost everyone will still stand there looking at her with blank stares and shrugging.

The attitude of the laterborns seems to be, "Yup, you're right. Something ought to be done about this. I wonder who'll be the one to do it."

The firstborn often makes promises to herself: *I'm not going to be the one to do that project this time. It's about time someone else does their share of the work.*

23

But then the deadline looms and the project still isn't done. It doesn't bother anyone but the firstborn, who is task oriented and perfectionistic. So what is the firstborn's reaction? "Oh, all right," she says in disgust, "I'll do it." She does it—and she does it well.

Then the firstborn goes home. She sees everything that needs to be done at home and starts feeling overwhelmed. She tells herself, *I'm not doing it. Yes, I can see that the trash needs to be taken out, but I'm not going to do it. Let someone else do it.*

For three days she'll go around the house, saying to herself, *I'm not going to take it out. It's not that big a deal, but it's a matter of principle.* Pretty soon every wastebasket in the house is overflowing, and there are three big, aromatic bags full of garbage sitting on the floor in the kitchen. It doesn't seem to bother anyone else in the family, but it really, *really* bothers her. She fights against giving in . . . fights it and fights it and fights it . . . then, at last, gives in. *I can't stand it anymore. Okay, I give up—I'll take the trash out.*

> I can't stand it anymore. Okay, I give up—I'll take the trash out.

Now, did anyone else force her to take the trash out? No. (Chances are, the fact there was garbage in the kitchen probably didn't register high on the priority scale of the other birth orders in the family.) All the pressure came from within—from the firstborn's perfectionistic tendencies. She could just hear her father saying, "Victoria, how *could* you leave such a mess?" And those mental tapes ran on and on until she just had to do something about the mess in her kitchen.

For firstborns, taking out the trash can become a symbol of taking on the world. As an American Airlines flight attendant once told me, "We are trained to take trash from people—and still smile and say thank you."

The firstborn child will most likely be the one to notice when the dog needs to be fed and when the hamster needs to have fresh water and a clean cage. She'll be more likely to keep her room neat and clean, and this can lead to some loud battles if she's sharing a room with a less organized younger sibling.

In a marriage the firstborn partner will be the one who tends to notice when the walls need painting, when the furniture needs to be replaced, and when the grass needs mowing.

How can firstborns, middleborns, and lastborns be so different? And how did it happen?

It All Started Back in the Den

Cubs can come out of the same den, yet they can be so different. Amazing, isn't it? Take a look at the family you grew up in. If you're a firstborn, you can bet that the baby of the

---

The Axioms of the Firstborn

"Everyone depends on me."
"I can't get away with anything."
"It's tough being the oldest."
"I was never allowed to be a child."
"If I don't do it, it won't get done."
"If I don't do it, it won't get done right."
"I never said I wanted to be a role model."
"Boy, if I acted the way you do . . ."
"Mom never let me do that when I was your age."
"Why do I have to do it? They never do anything around here."

---

family has a completely different personality from you. And if you have your own children, the same exact thing is true. Just why is that?

How can children who grew up in the same environment not act the same?

It's a misconception to think that children who grow up in the same family grow up in the same environment. They don't at all. The parents are the same, the house is the same, and the neighborhood and schools may be the same, but the relationships within the family are entirely different.

Let's say that Mom has told Lisa, the secondborn in the family but the firstborn girl, that she is not allowed to ride her bicycle to the corner grocery store, and she'll be grounded if she does. But then along comes big brother Al, who's feeling a bit mean today, and he tells Lisa that he wants her to ride to the corner store and buy him a candy bar. If she doesn't do it, he's going to clobber her. (Now, if he's a decent big brother, he wouldn't really hit his sister, but I doubt there's an older brother anywhere who hasn't threatened to do so at one time or another.) So poor sis is caught in the middle of a situation she can't win.

This is the sort of environment she finds herself in every day as the firstborn daughter: wanting to please her big brother (even if he does have a mean streak), helping take care of her little brother (and protect him from their older brother), *and* following her parents' rules.

And what about little brother? His environment is shaped not only by his relationships with his older siblings but also by the footprints they have left for him to follow. When he goes to school, he may hear the teachers say, "I certainly hope you're going to be a good student—just like your older brother

26

and sister." Or he may hear them murmur, "I hope this one isn't going to be a troublemaker like his brother."

Either way, the youngest one is being prejudged. A certain behavior is going to be expected of him, and it will be tough for him to prove that he is his own person.

See what I mean about children from the same family growing up in totally different environments?

Esteemed psychologist Alfred Adler had this to say about the effect that birth order can and often does have on our lives:

> The position in the family leaves an indelible stamp upon the style of life. Every difficulty of development is caused by rivalry and lack of cooperation in the family. If we look around at our social life and ask why rivalry and competition is its most obvious aspect—indeed, not only at our social life but at our whole world—then we must recognize that people are everywhere pursuing the goal of being conqueror, of overcoming and surpassing others. This goal is the result of training in early childhood, of the rivalries and competitive striving of children who have not felt themselves an equal part of their whole family.[1]

> It's a misconception to think that children who grow up in the same family grow up in the same environment. They don't at all.

Few things shape your life as much as your birth order. That's why I've spent years studying it and helping others understand it. And happily, it's gained enough national attention that *Time* magazine recently ran a cover story on the power of birth order.[2] I find it fascinating that *Time* magazine just discovered it, since I've been in the trenches of birth order study for over forty years, even before I wrote *The Birth Order Book: Why You Are the Way You Are* in 1985.

Writer Jeffrey Kluger gives some good examples of sibling pairs who, though they grew up in the same homes, went in completely different directions. For example, there's Elliott Roosevelt, younger sibling of Teddy Roosevelt. Elliott struggled with alcohol, morphine addiction, and depression. Teddy authored numerous books and became president of the United States. Donald Nixon, younger brother of former president Richard Nixon, got in trouble for wangling funds from billionaire Howard Hughes. Roger Clinton, younger half brother of former president Bill Clinton, spent a year in jail on a cocaine conviction. Billy Ripken, a major league infielder, is little noticed when the press swarms around his older brother and Hall of Famer Cal Ripken. Then there's Tisa Farrow, an actress few have heard of from her 1979 film, *Zombie*, and her better-known older sister, Mia.[3]

> Whatever the firstborn in a family is like, the secondborn will go in the entirely opposite direction. And the baby of the family will be a party waiting to happen.

What made these younger siblings less gifted or more prone to trouble? For the answer, take a look at the family you grew up in. Who was the responsible one? Who was the "party waiting to happen"? Who was the rebellious child who went his own way?

After thirty-four years as a psychologist counseling families, I can guarantee you that whatever the firstborn in a

28

family is like, the secondborn will go in the entirely opposite direction. And the baby of the family will be a party waiting to happen.

It's all about birth order—the order in which each child was born in your family. You see, with the arrival of each child, a family changes. All parents practice on the firstborn, aka "guinea pig." As the second child (if there is one) comes along, parents either get better at their parenting skills or, frankly, wear down. By the time they get to the lastborn, they're parenting pros (or completely worn out), so they're not as uptight.

Kids are smart critters—they're always looking to whoever is above them on the family tree. A firstborn or only child gets her cues from her parents. A secondborn looks at the firstborn. And the baby? He watches what his firstborn *and* middleborn siblings do and learns how to work the system. It doesn't take long before he's a pro.

Different Strokes for Different Folks

I've written an entire book about birth order, brilliantly called *The Birth Order Book*. (I wanted to call it *Abel Had It Coming*, but that didn't go over well with the powers that be in the publishing world, so they came up with a more creative title.) It explains the birth orders and their characteristics in detail. It's well worth the read, because it will help you understand not only yourself but also your family members, friends, co-workers, and neighbors. Since there's such a wealth of material in that book, there's no need to refer in detail to the different birth orders here. However, for the sake of contrasting the firstborn traits with the middleborn and lastborn traits, I'll give a quick summary here.

Think about the members of your family as you were growing up. Think also of any children you have now. What personalities and gifts do they have? What strengths and weaknesses? How do they fit into these characteristics of birth order?

Firstborns and Only Children

Reliable and conscientious, they tend to be list makers and black-and-white thinkers. They have a keen sense of right and wrong and believe there is a "right way" to do things. They are natural leaders and achievement oriented.

Only children take those characteristics a step further. Books are their best friends. They act mature beyond their years—they are little adults by age 7 or 8. They work independently. And they can't understand why kids in other families fight.

Middleborns

They're the hardest to pin down of all the birth orders, but I'll hang my hat on this truth: middleborns will be the opposite of the child above them in the family. If the firstborn is very conventional, the second will be unconventional. Middle children walk to the beat of a different drummer. They are competitive, loyal, and big on friendships. Donald Trump, Steve Forbes, and Bill Gates are all middle children.

Being stuck in the middle is no picnic. It means not getting as much attention as the oldest and youngest children.

The oldest is special simply because he's oldest. Mom and Dad would stand transfixed around his crib each night just watching him sleep. They could hardly believe that their union had produced this new life—and such a beautiful new life it was. This parenthood business was all so new and exciting.

As for the youngest? He's special because he's the baby, and he'll always be the baby, even if he's 6'4" and weighs 245 pounds.

Being the middle child means living in a sort of anonymous haziness. But that's not all bad. If a middle child is anonymous, he can get away with occasional laziness and indifference. He's not pushed as hard or expected to accomplish quite as much as the one who came before him. The drawback is that without being pushed, he may never fulfill his potential. But it's better than being pushed too hard and asked to perform beyond his capabilities. And that's what often happens to the firstborn.

The middle child of the family is often the negotiator who tries to keep the peace. It's no wonder, then, that middle children often grow up to be well-adjusted and monogamous adults.

Lastborns

These social, outgoing creatures have never met a stranger. They are uncomplicated, spontaneous, humorous, and high on people skills. To them, life's a party. They're most likely to get away with murder and least likely to be punished. They often retain their pet name. I oughta know; my wife calls me Leemie. But because she's a firstborn, if she gets a little too bossy, I often call her by her given name, Sandra.

But there's also a flip side to being the youngest. I know about that too. Although they're the little star in the family constellation, lastborns have a few trials of their own. It's no fun being the smallest, because it means they spend a lot of their time wearing hand-me-downs that are ragged, incredibly out of style, or too big. Being the youngest also means that they get picked on from time to time and maybe get called an unflattering nickname. My siblings called me "crater head" because of deep scars left by a bout with chicken pox. I also took my share of pounding at the hands of my older brother, Jack. I used to refer to him sarcastically as God—as in, "Oh, I see God's home," or, "Hey, God, you have a telephone call!" As a kid, I walked around with perpetually sore shoulders. Jack didn't have a punching bag, but he did have those shoulders, and he seemed to punch them nearly every chance he got.

But I might as well confess that there are some pretty good things about being the youngest too. For one thing, although big brother may pick on you, he's not about to let anyone else push you around. If a bully is picking on you at school, usually all you have to do is sic your big brother—or, in my case, my firstborn sister—on him, and your worries will be over. My sister, Sally, remembers that when she was twelve, she marched up the front steps of a house, rang the doorbell, and confronted a 38-year-old woman whose son was picking on her baby brother—namely, me. She made it clear that if the bully didn't stop picking on kids half his age, she was personally going to turn him inside out.

That's the way it is with firstborns. Mom and Dad may think they're in charge, but the firstborn knows better, and so does the youngest sibling.

Being the youngest means getting away with a lot of things too—like murder. Why? Because no one's going to kill the youngest. Mom and Dad are never as strict with the youngest—probably because they're too tired from making all the older boys and girls toe the line.

But What About . . . ?

"Dr. Leman," you might be saying, "my kids don't fit into those lists. My middleborn acts like a firstborn, and my firstborn acts like a lastborn. I'm not sure I buy this firstborn business, because it sounds just a little too pat to me. There's got to be a catch."

You hit the nail on the head. Your kids don't fit into those lists because there's more to birth order than meets the eye. You could be an eighth-born child and have a firstborn personality. Or you could be a third-born child and have a first-born personality. Why? Read on, and we'll put the pieces of the puzzle together.

2

Who's on First?

Just because you're the first child born in a family, does that make you the firstborn? Here's why . . . or why not.

A woman from Kentucky approached me at one of my seminars and said she was stumped about "this birth order thing." She plunged right in to what troubled her about it all. "I don't understand, Dr. Leman. There are nine children in my family. My oldest brother should have firstborn tendencies, but he doesn't act at all like a firstborn. So who is the firstborn in my family?"

I like a good challenge, so I listed the children in order of their ordinal (birth) position:

1.   Boy
2. Girl

3. Girl  (the woman I spoke to was this child)
4.   Boy
5. Girl
6.   Boy
7.   Boy
8.   Boy
9.   Boy

"Did you refer to your four younger brothers as 'the little boys'?" I asked.

She nodded.

"So where would you divide your family into groups?" I asked. "Go ahead and draw the lines." So she divided the family into the following groups:

1.   Boy
2. Girl
3. Girl (the woman I spoke to was this child)

———

4.   Boy
5. Girl

———

6.   Boy
7.   Boy
8.   Boy
9.   Boy

I wasn't surprised. When I ask a person from a large family to draw the lines between "the big ones," "the little ones," and himself/herself, that person can tell you exactly where those lines go.

In large families, there is always more than one functional firstborn.

For example:

The first subfamily had no middle child.

1. Boy was a firstborn who didn't act like a firstborn, according to his sister
2. Girl (the first daughter born in the family) was the firstborn daughter, so she acted like it
3. Girl (the woman I spoke to) was the apple of her daddy's eye, so she ended up being the baby of the family

The second subfamily had no middle child.

4. Boy had strong firstborn traits
5. Girl had strong firstborn traits

The third subfamily had one middle child. Can you find him?

6. Boy had firstborn traits
7. Boy
8. Boy
9. Boy had baby-of-the-family traits

In the last grouping, the middleborn child is, most likely, the second or third son of the bottom four. He's easy to pick out. He's the negotiator who attempts to smooth the oceans of life. The other child will either be looking up to the firstborn boy, trying to be like him, or be walking around with his underwear in his back pocket (which would confirm baby-of-the-family status for me). The key to remember is that, no matter what the second boy in that last grouping does, the third boy will go in a completely different direction. That's why in this family of nine, there is only one middle child.

Who's the firstborn in your family? Could it be that whoever's third in line is really the one who's the firstborn?

Some researchers with PhDs diss the whole birth order theory because they take into consideration *only* the ordinal position or "rank"—who came out of the womb first. They completely disregard the whole phenomenon of the functional firstborn.

But I have been convinced for years, and have seen the truth of this theory time and time again, that birth order deals not only with the *ordinal* position of the child but also with the *functional* position of the child.

There are many variables that affect the functional position of each child in the family. Let me explain.

Variables That Play into Birth Order

Large Families

A case in point, as explained above with the family of the woman from Kentucky: the larger the family, the more possibilities of having subunits within the family.

Male or Female

You don't have to be a rocket scientist to realize that if there are four boys and one girl in your family, there's something unique about one of your kids. Pay special attention to opposite-sex messages. How does Daddy treat daughter? How does Mommy treat son? If Daddy overprotects older

Schnooky because she's a girl, she may end up with lastborn characteristics. If Mommy coddles older son because he's a boy, she might produce a baby of the family.

Or both children could have firstborn traits. That's because each is playing the functional role for either the first male or the first female child in the family. For example, my son, Kevin, is surrounded by four sisters, but he has a firstborn personality, and that makes sense. He's the first and only son in the family.

Age Gap of Five Years or More

Whenever there is at least a five-year gap between same-sex children, you can draw a line psychologically and start another functional family.

Anna, 12   (firstborn girl)

_____

Claire, 5   (firstborn girl)

Mary, 2   (baby girl)

Physical/Mental Differences or Challenges

Let's say you have two sons. Your firstborn, Fletcher, is 5 feet, and little "Moose" is 5'6". Fletcher is also average-looking and not athletic. Moose is handsome and athletic. Sad to say, it's a shallow world we live in, and that will make a difference in the way your sons are treated. If you're shorter, people assume you're younger. And average-looking, less athletic people don't seem to be noticed as much as their more athletic, good-looking counterparts. So your sons' birth order will likely be reversed. Why? Because of the way they are perceived. Ditto for a secondborn daughter who is prettier in the world's eyes than the firstborn daughter.

If you have an oldest child or second son or daughter with Down syndrome, how does that affect the birth order? Most likely it will be reversed in your children. If your Down child is a firstborn, the secondborn will not only show signs of a firstborn personality but will also be protective of his or her Down syndrome sibling. Interestingly, this new first-born is much more sensitive to the cruelty of others who don't understand how loving and kind and wonderful Down children can be. Down children come without a critical eye or any baggage. They extend their hands and hearts in unrestrained love.

I'll never forget what happened several years ago at the Special Olympics. The smiley-faced competitors were lined up for the 100-yard dash. At the starting signal, they all took off, intent on the goal of the finish line and winning the prize.

As one of the runners rounded a corner, he fell. Tears streamed down his cheeks as he sat on the track, feeling defeated, worthless, and hurt.

What happened next is one of the most memorable moments in sports history. *All* of the Special Olympics runners turned back toward the little boy. They gathered around him and linked arms around him, and together they walked to the finish line.

There was not a dry eye in the stadium.

Why was this particular moment so memorable? Because it was so counter to our human nature of selfishly going after our own goals. The runners may not have won any individual medals that day, but they did what was most important—they ran the race *together.* And that made them all winners, not only in the eyes of others but in their own hearts, where it really matters.

Having a child with physical or mental challenges affects not only birth order but the way everyone in the family looks at life. Shelli, mom of 11-year-old Tate, a boy with Down syndrome, says, "I'm convinced that it has made my husband, myself, and our two other children better people, just because we have the gift of Tate."

Blended Families

Family structure also plays into the variables of birth order. For example, is your family a blended family? Is it made up of two families that came together as a result of divorce, abandonment, or the death of one or more spouses?

Take Barack Obama, for instance. He has eight half siblings (seven of them living) by four other marriages or relationships his parents had. His father, Barack Obama Sr., had two children by a woman he married in Kenya. After they divorced, Obama Sr. married Obama's mother, after which Obama Jr. was born. After the couple divorced, Obama Sr. married an American woman and had two more sons. That marriage ended in divorce, after Obama Sr. resumed his relationship with his first wife and then had two other sons. He later had another son by a woman with whom he was

> As firstborns, neither is going to say, "Okay, whatever you think," or, "You go ahead and call the shots." Nuh-uh. That's not the way things are going to be.

involved. Obama Jr's mother had a daughter from a second marriage.[1]

If your family is blended, then you will have some particular challenges that are unique to blended families—challenges that have everything to do with your firstborn children.

Remember the old slogan for American Express? "Don't leave home without it!" That's true of birth order. You don't need a PhD to figure out that if a 13-year-old and a 12-year-old (both firstborns from their birth families) are together, they'll clash. Neither is going to willingly surrender his birth order. (Unless, of course, one of them is like Esau, who was so hungry that he sold his birthright to his younger brother for a bowl of porridge. It probably wasn't the best business transaction he ever made, and look what it led to.)

As firstborns, neither is going to say, "Okay, whatever you think," or, "You go ahead and call the shots." Nuh-uh. That's not the way things are going to be. Rather, it'll be like two mountain goats butting their heads to vie for territorial rights, and you're going to hear the clash of their horns from miles away.

And what are you thinking? *What happened? They really seemed to like each other before we got married.* After you and your new spouse walked down that flower-strewn aisle, everything seemed to change . . . for the worst.

The reality is, everyone in the family has been hurt by that divorce, abandonment, or death. When you try to put together the happy Brady Bunch—his and hers—a natural calamity is awaiting you if your children are anywhere close in age (for example, yours are 13 and 10, and his are 12, 11, and 9). However, if your children are 16 and 17, and his are 4 and 5, that's an easier blend. Those children are less likely to be in each others' faces, competing for your time and attention.

Also, if your children are being shuffled back and forth between your and your ex's residences, they may feel jealous and hurt that their new brothers and sisters get your attention all the time, while they get to see you only every other weekend or for two months in the summer.

Imagine what goes through your child's mind. If your prior relationship ended in divorce, it's only natural for your child to test the new relationship. By doing so, she's saying, *Hey, are you guys for real? Are you going to stay together? I don't want to go through a divorce again. It hurt too much.*

What if your child's parent died? Don't you think your child will fear losing another parent? *If I don't learn to love him, I won't lose him. I never want to be hurt again*, she thinks.

You see, under the foundation of the new family is a layer of anger, bitterness, jealousy, competition, hurt, and anger. Note how I laid out the words in that sentence: I used *anger* twice—once at the front and once at the back. You have to understand that everyone in a blended family comes with some emotional scars and baggage.

But if you accept these realities and work to understand what is going on in your child's mind, you can better form a plan *as a couple*. This is particularly important when it comes to your firstborn children.

Guess what child in the family was closest to what went wrong in the first marriage? The firstborn! Ever see an ice cutter on a big lake? It plows through the ice that would do damage to other boats. But in the process, it takes a lot of hits and gets physically battered. Your firstborn is the ice cutter in the lake of life. She's the one who's been most battered in the process. She may not be able to explain to you how she feels, but that damage will show in the ways she interacts with everyone in your family.

When your children are at war with each other, what usually happens? In a blended family, Mama and Papa Bear tend to protect their own cubs. But once you pick sides in a blended family, it's over. You're done. You become just two separate families living together, protecting their own territory.

The reality is that it takes three to seven years of patience, flexibility, humor, and determination to blend a family. And, like anything else in life, how well the family blends depends on your awareness of the issues involved.

If you're considering blending your family (you haven't walked down that flower-strewn aisle yet), here are some things to think about:

1. Look before you leap. Just because your children seem to like that person you're spending time with doesn't mean they will accept him as a new daddy or her as a new mommy.

2. Consider the ages of the children. Are they close or farther apart? That will make all the difference in how they try to compete (or not compete) with each other. As children leave the home, it becomes easier to blend families. If the children are nearing the end of high school, for example, you might be wise to wait a year or two to marry until they are in college and/or out of the nest.

3. If your first spouse died, realize, as expert Harold Bloomfield says, "The children idealize the memory of the dead parent. When a widow/widower remarry, the loyalty issues for children can be even more difficult

than after divorce."[2] No person can "take the place" of that deceased parent, so no one should try. But you can work to establish a friendship and a position of respect that, depending on the age of your child, may eventually grow into your child accepting that person as a new mommy or daddy.

If you're already in a blended family, here are some tips to help you navigate the sometimes rocky waters. (For more advice, see my book *Living in a Stepfamily without Getting Stepped On*.[3])

1. As a couple, take a stand together on *everything*. The children need to see that there is no "yours" and "mine"; everything is "ours." Do not let your children drive a wedge between you. You need to function as a unit, not as separate heads of two families. Your children will try you, sure—if for no other reason than that they've been hurt by the marriage process before, and they want to know if this marriage is for real and if it will last. Frankly, it's not that they want to rain on your parade; it's just that they are so miserable, so why should you be happy? They are, in effect, asking, *Will you fold up like you did on the first marriage? If I buy into this family thing, will I be hurt like I was when I found out you and Dad were divorcing?*
2. Always talk things through with everyone concerned. Have family meetings where each member's voice can be heard.
3. Don't make decisions that affect others in the family without checking with them first.
4. Stick to this family rule like glue: don't touch other people's belongings without their permission.

5. Each family member's individuality is important. Each member should be treated as an individual.
6. Each member should pull his or her own fair share of the family workload.
7. Remember that your home is a *home*, not a hotel. No one has the right to come and go as they please. All rules should be based on mutual respect and love.

Recently I had a conversation with a couple who had successfully blended their family. I asked them, "What advice would you give a family that was just beginning to blend?"

They smiled at each other and answered in unison, "Stand united. Stand shoulder to shoulder."

And then they shared, "We've really grown to love each other by sticking to a couple simple principles: (1) Insist on respect and kindness—always. But don't force your kids to love each other. Love doesn't demand its own way. (2) Don't step into your children's relational battles. Encourage them to solve their own problems."

The other important key to their success? Both spouses shared a common faith that became a strong foundation for their new family.

> Blending a family can have its own particular challenges, but there's good news. Many a blended family out there not only has made it but has flourished. Yours can too.

Blending a family can have its own particular challenges, but there's good news. Many a blended family out there not only has made it but has flourished. Yours can too.

When struggles occur, don't pick sides; be task oriented. If there's a problem between the children, let them work it out.

Keep the ball in their court. Don't be the heavyweight who steps between them and solves their problem for them.

Keep your "couple view." This is especially hard for women, since Mama Bear's first consideration is always going to be, "What about *my* little cub?" If you're the male in this blended family and you didn't have children previously, you have to understand that you need to love Mama Bear *and* her cubs. If Mama Bear ain't happy, then you ain't gonna be happy, and Mr. Happy ain't gonna be happy. Know what I'm saying?

Don't let guilt from your past decisions and failures stop you from acting in everyone's best interests. With an awareness of the issues and a policy of standing firm together, of making all decisions in conjunction with your spouse, and of insisting on respect as the foundation of your home, you too can experience the benefits of living in the kind of family you've dreamed of.

Adoption

If you adopt an infant, there is usually no effect on birth order. However, keep the age gap in mind. If the child you adopt is the youngest of four but there's a gap greater than five years between her and your next older child, you're essentially rearing your adopted child as a firstborn or only child. And she will have firstborn and/or only-child personality traits.

One family we know just adopted a 2-year-old from Guatemala. He was happily welcomed home by the family's two other children: a college-age daughter and a twelfth-grade daughter. This situation works well for the family since he's the firstborn son, and his siblings are both daughters and more than five years older than him, so there is no friction of competition between the siblings.

If you have adopted a child, blessings on you and your home for choosing this gift of love. As adoptive parents who are friends of mine say, "But, Doc, *we* are the ones who truly received the gift. We can't imagine life without our daughter from China."

If that little bundle of joy is young, she may not yet have much "private logic"—the way she looks at and interprets actions, words, and events. And most likely she will easily fit into the flow of your family since she will not remember most of her prior surroundings.

But if you have adopted a child five years of age or older, realize that her private logic has already been greatly formed. If she has been abused, used, neglected, or abandoned, you will deal with these issues for years to come as you parent her. As issues arise, talk with your child about them. Soothe her fears. Remind her that she is an important part of your family.

But there's also a caveat here. Remember that no one person in the family—or her needs—is more important than any other person. Some adopted children, if they have been hurt in the past, may lash out against other children in your family. They can turn your family dynamics upside down as you all adjust to your life together.

For example, one family came to me because their adopted 4-year-old kept slapping the other children (ages 7, 9, and 10) when they wanted a hug from their mother. What was the 4-year-old saying by his behavior? "She's *mine*, and you can't have her. I've never had anyone who was truly mine, and I won't let her out of my sight, nor will I share her."

Once the family was aware of what the behavior meant, they could explain to the other children what was going on (which helped the other children in their perspective, since this had been going on for a year already) and then work on the behavior with the little boy. He was told that such behavior was not allowed in the family and that he would be put in a time-out chair if he tried to slap or did slap one of his siblings. He was assured of his parents' love, and of his safe position as one of the members of the family, with multiple hugs and verbal affirmations. But the parents no longer allowed that little boy to be in charge of the family dynamics. Think the stress level in that family went down? You bet. And the other children started smiling again too.

Sure, there will be initial adjustment times when the new family member who comes to your home will need more parental time and attention. After all, everything is completely new to that child, and new can be scary. Also, if your child is an infant or toddler, she won't be able to do many things (if anything) for herself. But even in that initial adjustment, do not allow the new family member to start running the family. You're the parent; you should still be in charge. And the rule of your home needs to be love and respect for *all* family members.

Never hesitate to seek additional help, if needed, from a trusted mentor, other adoptive parents who are farther down the pike in their experience, adoption groups who regularly discuss issues such as the ones you face, or a professional counselor. You'll be glad you did, because your whole family will benefit.

It's Not About the Womb, It's About the Relationship

What makes a person a firstborn? It's not about who came out of the womb first (even with twins) or who arrives first in the home via adoption. It's the *relationship* between the child and adult that makes the person a firstborn—or not. That's why I'll be devoting all of chapter 6 to the most important variable of all—the kind of relationship you had with your parent(s), and how that relationship not only influenced you then but has everything to do with who you are now.

Did you have a parent who was a chronic flaw picker, who could spot anything you did wrong (translation: anything not according to that parent's perfect standards) at fifty paces? Have you, as a result, become a chronic flaw picker of your own flaws and others'?

Interview with a Firstborn Skeptic

Does any of this ring true for you?

Firstborn: You say firstborns are supposed to be superior in organization and driven, and I'm not. All you'd have to do is take a look at my desk, and you'd realize just how wrong you are.

Dr. Leman: Really? Well, if it's that bad, how do you ever know where anything is?

Firstborn: Oh, it's easy. It may not look like it, but I know exactly where to find anything I want.

Dr. Leman: So you're not as disorganized as you would appear to be at first glance. If you know where everything is, that means you're fairly well organized, doesn't it?

Firstborn: Well . . . yeah, I suppose so.

Dr. Leman: So, what do you do at this desk anyway? What's your occupation?

Firstborn: I'm an architect.

Dr. Leman *(nodding)*: An architect. Hmm . . . most of the architects I've known were either firstborn or only children. An architect has to be very careful about his work, doesn't he?

continued—

Firstborn: You bet he does. There's no room for mistakes or for being even a little off the mark.

Dr. Leman: That's another striking characteristic of firstborns. Whatever they do, they do as well as they can. You don't hear firstborns saying things like, "Aw, that's good enough," or, "It's not perfect, but it'll do." You're sounding more and more like a firstborn to me.

Firstborn: I'm not sure I'm ready to buy it—especially the bit about my sloppy desk really being organized. Seems to me that if I were as organized and efficient as you say I am, I'd have a place for everything, and I'd keep everything in its place.

Dr. Leman: Believe it or not, people who have sloppy desks are sometimes more concerned with being perfect than people who appear on the surface to be neat and organized. The person who has the sloppy desk may be what I refer to as a "discouraged perfectionist." He wants everything in his life to be perfect, and because he knows it never can be, he tends to leave things half done or not done at all. In other words, he's afraid to attempt things that he knows he can't do perfectly.

Firstborn: What about this? I have a younger sister—the third of three children in my family—and according to what you say, she's more like a firstborn than I am. She's always been the best at anything she's ever tried: she was student body president in high school, president of her sorority in college, editor of her college newspaper, and president of the National Honor Society, and she earned a law degree from a prestigious university. She's eight years younger than I am, and she's leaving me in her dust. I mean, from everything I know about birth order, I thought lastborns were supposed to be happy-go-lucky types who take life as it comes. I thought they were supposed to have fun in life and not push themselves so hard.

Dr. Leman: That's true. But your sister may not be a lastborn at all. She may, in fact, be a firstborn, just like you.

Firstborn: What are you talking about? How could she possibly be a firstborn?

Dr. Leman: Would I be correct in assuming that the child in between the two of you is a male?

Firstborn: You would.

Dr. Leman: And how much younger than you is he?

continued—

Firstborn: Three years.

Dr. Leman: All of this makes perfect sense to me. As a matter of fact, your baby sister is a firstborn on two accounts. First of all, she's a firstborn because she's the only girl in the family. Now, that doesn't mean she had to take on all the characteristics of a firstborn; it just means that was a good possibility. The second reason she's a firstborn is that there is a five-year gap between the middle child and her. Whenever there is a gap of five years or more, the next-born child can be considered a firstborn.

Firstborn: Now I'm really confused. I was under the impression there could be only one firstborn in every family. Now you're telling me there can be several?

Dr. Leman: That's right. Usually there will be just one firstborn or at the most two, due to sex differences, but if the children in a particular family are spaced far enough apart, it's possible that there could be four or even five children who take on the characteristics of firstborns. I doubt that you'll find very many families where there are several children all spaced five years or more apart, but it could happen.

Firstborn: Why does age make such a big difference?

Dr. Leman: Primarily because it lessens the competition between siblings. Your brother is, what, three years younger than you? That's close enough so that he probably had many of the same teachers you had. When he came to school, people remembered you and your accomplishments, and he was under pressure to measure up. You see, the firstborn tends to look at his mother and father and want to be like them. They're the only role models he has, and that's one reason so many firstborn sons follow in their father's footsteps and go into the same careers.

But then little brother comes along, and he has not only Mom and Dad to follow but a big brother too. And he sees his brother doing a pretty good job of living up to Mom and Dad's expectations. Whoa—it looks like he'll have to find his own way to make everyone notice him. Let's say, for instance, that you were pretty good in sports.

Firstborn: I was.

Dr. Leman: Okay, so that means your younger brother probably found it difficult to compete against you on the athletic level. Unless he happened to be born with a fair amount of natural athletic ability, he probably would have looked for another way to excel.

continued—

Firstborn: Yeah, he was really into music. Played guitar in a rock 'n' roll band.

Dr. Leman: So your brother is more of a lastborn than your sister is. It's typical of lastborns to seek out the limelight. They love to be the center of attention—and I'd guess that was one thing your brother got out of playing in a rock band. Lastborns, you see, often have a hard time getting attention. There's not much they can do that their older brothers and sisters haven't done before, so from the moment they come into this world, they're looking for a way to get their fair share of attention—and most of them can never get enough. For instance, do you remember the guy who was always the class clown in your school?

Firstborn: Harry Wilson.

Dr. Leman: Well, old Harry was probably a lastborn. Class clowns almost always are, especially if they come from larger, overachieving families. If little Harry has two older brothers who are whizzes in sports and music and two older sisters who are top-notch artistically and scholastically, well, that doesn't leave a whole lot for him to claim as his own. So he's more likely to become the show-off or the rebel as a means of gaining attention.

Firstborn: My brother, Charlie, was always up to something. One time he told everyone in his Latin class to bring an alarm clock. About twelve of the twenty-five classmates did . . . and all twelve of those clocks went off right in the middle of the final exam.

Dr. Leman: Typical behavior for a lastborn. I bet Charlie was a persuasive guy too. He probably had lots of friends and was good at getting them to go along with him on things. Because lastborns are generally outgoing and personable, they make terrific salespeople. What does your brother do for a living?

Firstborn: Well, you've described his personality pretty well, but you've missed it on the career. He's not a salesman—he's an account executive for an ad agency.

Dr. Leman: But isn't "account executive" a fancy term for "salesman"? You have to sell your clients on your proposals, don't you? And besides, the entire purpose of advertising is to increase sales.

Firstborn: I suppose so. But I still don't quite get it. From what you're telling me, there are only so many personality types in the world—firstborns, middleborns, and lastborns.

continued—

53

Dr. Leman: And only children. But only children are a hybrid version of firstborns, since they share many similarities.

Firstborn: It's just hard to believe birth order plays such an important role in shaping the personality. I mean, I look around and see lots of different types of people and personalities.

Dr. Leman: I never said that birth order was the only thing shaping the human personality. There are a tremendous number of variables in the equation that make you who you are. And even in birth order there are variables involved. For instance, consider the firstborn male who has younger brothers. He'll be the tough boss-of-bosses type, the kingpin. He'll be an achiever and probably do important things, but he won't understand women particularly well and might not make the best husband the world has ever seen.

A firstborn male who has younger sisters will probably be more sensitive. He'll still be an achiever, but he'll have a more compassionate, softer side that he'll have learned through relating to his sisters. He's going to be more sensitive to women and their needs, and he'll do better in marriage.

However, because he has always been older than his sisters and has been the one to stand up for them and protect them, he'll tend to be a bit chauvinistic and believe that women need his help and protection.

Then there's the firstborn male who has an older sister or sisters. He should have an even better understanding of the worth and abilities of women.

The firstborn female who has only sisters is going to view life in one way, skewed to a particularly feminine point of view, whereas the firstborn female with younger brothers will have a different outlook.

Then there's the only child. I can look at volumes of research and tell you how he'll tend to approach life—but there are also many variables involved. One is why he's an only child. Is it because his parents were physically unable to have other children? If so, they'll treat their one precious child in a particular way, especially if they desperately wanted those other children they could not have.

Or perhaps little Junior's an only child because his parents took one look at his face when he was born, ran screaming from the delivery room, and swore they'd never have another baby if this was the result. Or perhaps his parents planned for only one child, figuring that this was the

continued—

only way they could afford to give him the best of everything—the best toys, the best clothes, the best education. You see how all these things would alter the way they dealt with their child, and how that, in turn, would alter his approach to life?

Firstborn: Yes . . . I see what you're saying.

Dr. Leman: There's nothing at all magical about birth order. It's not set in concrete that if you're a firstborn you're going to act one way, and if you're not you're going to act another way. Birth order has to do with the way our parents relate to us, how we interact with our siblings, the sex of our siblings, the economic status of our families, where we live, etc. All of these things go into the makeup of the family zoo.

Firstborn: I'm going to have to think about this for a while, put it all together in my head.

Dr. Leman *(laughing)*: I'd be surprised if you reacted any other way. Firstborns aren't leapers; they are cautious and take calculated risks. So it makes sense that you want to sleep on it before you move forward. Take your time and think about it, and we'll talk later.

Because all firstborns are particularly susceptible to criticism due to their own perfectionistic tendencies, this variable—the critical eye—is the single greatest determiner for whether you will succeed or fail as a firstborn at home, at school, at work, and in your relationships. It's well worth paying attention to.

You Be the Detective

Now you be the detective. Why would the following famous people be considered firstborns (or in three cases, only children)? (This is great material for a discussion with friends or co-workers over lunch. Just wait for the intriguing questions they'll have, and you can explain everything you've learned thus far.)

Angelina Jolie—Has an older brother

Brad Pitt—Has a younger brother and sister

Jennifer Aniston—Has two half brothers

Matt LeBlanc—Has a half brother

Joan of Arc—Has three brothers

David Schwimmer—Has an older sister

Matthew Perry—Has a half brother and four half sisters

Ben Stiller—Has an older sister

Lindsay Lohan—Has a younger sister and two younger brothers

Ben Affleck—Has a younger brother

Reese Witherspoon—Has an older brother

Lauren Conrad—Has a younger sister and brother

Fascinating, isn't it?

But again, I know firstborns. You're analytical, you're logical, and you're skeptical. So I'm not surprised you're not convinced quite yet of the role that birth order plays in shaping your lives.

Consider this. More and more influential people—like CEOs and human resources staff—are beginning to pay close attention to birth order because they're realizing that some of their key decisions about staffing relate to it. They're convinced that it could save their businesses millions of dollars every year.

What if you could figure out which individuals would make the best salespeople, the best sales managers, the best assistants, etc.? Wouldn't that be worth something to you?

Psychologist Karl Konig summarized the importance of birth order very well: "The family constellation shapes the social behavior of man. It determines the way he reacts to other people, how he is able to make friends or not, the way he finds companionship and community with others. Even the choice of a husband or wife is deeply influenced by the facts of the family constellation."[4]

Birth order and its variables are extremely important in your makeup and in your success in life. Your birth order position (functional and ordinal) has profoundly affected you, whether you realize it or not.

Guess the Firstborn

Look back at page 18 to see your answers to which of these pairs the firstborn is.

1. Matt Damon or Ben Affleck
2. Florence Henderson (*Brady Brunch* mom) or Martha Stewart
3. Reese Witherspoon or Sheryl Crow
4. Ben Stiller or Billy Crystal
5. Angelina Jolie or Brad Pitt

How did you do? If you guessed Affleck, Stewart, Witherspoon, Stiller, and Jolie *and* Pitt (wait, I tricked you!), you're right. Ben Affleck has one younger brother. Brad Pitt has a younger brother and a younger sister.

But why are Reese Witherspoon, Angelina Jolie, and Martha Stewart considered firstborns, even though they all have an older brother? Because they are the first daughters in their families. Why would Ben Stiller be considered a firstborn, even though he's born second in his family? Because he's the first son. Ah, now you're getting it. . . .

3

The Firstborn Personality

Firstborns are achievers. They get things done . . .
but there's a flip side to always winning.

M y grandchildren are as different as night and day, and
I love them both to pieces. Little Conner takes his
Thomas the Train toys and lines them up perfectly. And when
I say perfectly, I mean perfectly. A mason laying a brick wall
could use Conner's imaginary line that is formed by the front
of his trains. Everything about Connor is precise and exact.
Not only does he establish a plumb line in construction, but
he'll take the trains and arrange them by color—blue ones
all together, red ones all together, yellow ones all together. At
his young age, he thinks in logical progression.

Then there's little Adeline, who's cute as the dickens but
walks around with her underwear in her back pocket, asking

for help at every turn. She's a natural little entertainer who can't help but make you laugh.

Which one do you think is the firstborn?

If you're a firstborn, you tend to have a discerning eye. You have great visual and emotional acuity—you're able to look at a situation and dissect it. You might do that spatially with numbers; just one look will tell you immediately if something is wrong. The rest of us (this baby of the family included) could have those numbers in front of us for months and not have an inkling that anything is wrong.

Firstborns are pretty special; they get things done. They are loaded with personality and character qualities that make them winners in life.

Laura Carter, founder of the First Born Girls Social Club, says,

> People refer to us as "bossy," but we are number one on speed dial if someone is in crisis or when someone wants a project done to tight specifications. We know how to take charge and move through the work. We know what to say and do to solve the problem. It comes naturally to us. It's what we've been primed to do since day one. It's not hard to tell in the short space of a conversation who is a firstborn and who is a lastborn. Like the time I was interviewing on a talk show and the cohost said to the host, "I'll take care of that for you, Bill." Guess who was the firstborn? That seems to be the role that firstborns take in the world. It should be the firstborn's slogan: "I'll take care of that for you."[1]

Interestingly, nearly all comedians (Stephen Colbert, Jay Leno, Chevy Chase, etc.) are babies of the family. (Bill Cosby is a rare exception—and he has his doctorate.) But who's behind them, getting them organized? You guessed it: firstborns.

Birth Order ID

Firstborns are easy to identify. If you interviewed people in numerous offices and asked the firstborns to raise their hands, guess who would? The ones continually striving to better themselves. The ones always looking for more ways for the company to be efficient and make a greater profit. The ones constantly analyzing and searching to make sense out of things. They're the movers and shakers, the ones who end up as the top managers and CEOs.

The middleborns would be the hardest to pin down—mainly because they are always in the middle. They will tend to be the mediators, the middle management, the worker bees. If the middle child came from a family with a discouraged firstborn perfectionist, the middle child may assume firstborn personality traits. But if he came out of a family where he followed a perfectionistic firstborn achiever, that middle child will feel like he can never measure up. And if he can't ever do well enough, he'll have either an "I don't care" attitude or an "I'll show you" attitude.

Where would the babies be? That's easy. Chatting over coffee in the break room. Yet these are the same babies who can make huge sales simply because of their charming nature. They are great talkers, have high social skills, and are very persuasive.

You see, there really is a place for all birth orders in the universe.

Laura Carter asked the firstborn women in her club the following questions:

If you were on a movie set and could have your choice of any roles, what would you be?

(a) actor
(b) camera person
(c) director
(d) assistant director

The answer? Everyone wanted to be the director.

If you were involved with athletics, what would you want to be?

(a) coach
(b) assistant coach
(c) cheerleader
(d) fan

The answer? Everyone wanted to be the coach.[2]

Natural Leader

Firstborns are natural leaders. They can rally the forces like no one else because they're confident and can immediately come up with "the plan."

Martin Luther King Jr., a firstborn son, organized marches in Selma, Alabama, that changed the nature of our country and ended segregation. He had the ability to organize and pass on "the dream." Whenever you see a clip of him, nine out of ten times you see him saying, "I have a dream." He set the bar high for African Americans, but he also walked the talk. He was there right alongside people.

King always said he would never forget his earliest childhood memory of being in a shoe store in Atlanta with his father. He remembered that when a clerk told his dad to go to the back of the store to be served—because he was black—his father walked out. That firstborn son followed his father's example in leadership and followed directly in his shoes in making a lasting impact on a nation.

Well-Organized

Firstborn Martha Stewart is a marvel. Look how she's taken something as simple as cooking and decorating and made a kingdom out of it. That wouldn't have happened without firstborn organizational and leadership skills, as well as communication skills.

Reliable

This is one of the benchmarks of a firstborn. From day one, they are taught to be reliable. Who does a parent call on when he or she needs a job done, and done right? The firstborn. Why? Because that child is reliable and will get the job done. Firstborns are reliable because they've been held to a higher standard all their lives. There's not a firstborn alive who hasn't said to her mom or dad, "You're not going to let him do that, are you? You never let *me* do that when I was his age."

Firstborns are always ready to pitch in and help because they've been groomed to do so. They have a high sense of what's right and what's wrong. There's not a lot of gray in the black and white of a firstborn's world.

Conscientious

Firstborns are conscientious because being conscientious is the right thing to do. They're the ones who take the grocery cart that's rolling around in the lot back into the store or pick up the receipt that fell on the pavement and throw it in the garbage. They wipe up the spilled coffee from the countertop at work or throw away the Styrofoam cup lying on the playground (all the middleborns and babies of the family have passed it by for days).

If I really want to know right off the bat if a client coming for a session with me is a firstborn, I slightly tilt one of the pictures in my office. Most firstborns will actually straighten out the picture for me because it bothers them. Other firstborns will go into the john on the airplane and will clean the washbasin that all the babies and middleborns have messed up.

> If I really want to know right off the bat if a client coming for a session with me is a firstborn, I slightly tilt one of the pictures in my office.

In other words, the automatic response of a firstborn is to right the ship. If I'm an employer, I want to hire someone conscientious because I'll sleep better at night. When that firstborn employee walks out of my retail store at night, he won't forget to lock the door. Chances are, when he gets to his car he'll ask himself, *Did I lock the door? Hmm, I'm not sure. Better go double-check.*

Now, the baby of the family? He's already zoomed off to meet his buddies at Starbucks, not giving the door another thought.

List Maker

My oldest daughter is an amazing list maker. I've watched her when she sorts things out at work, where she's a school principal. She'll first organize the papers and write things down (in alphabetical order, of course). Somehow in the tremendous amount of clutter that accumulates at the school, she has the keen ability to see through all the litter and confusion and to attack any problem in a logical, consistent, practical way. She can get through huge stacks in a short amount of time. She definitely inherited this quality of organization from her mother, not me.

The firstborn is the person who writes a list before she goes to the grocery store, then systematically gets everything on the list. The baby is the one who wanders aisle to aisle, looking for whatever looks good or he remembers he needs. When I get the grocery list from my wife, all the fruits are listed together and all the frozen foods are listed together. Yup, my wife's a firstborn.

Creatures of Habit

Firstborns don't like surprises. They like things to be orderly and organized. Just try tucking your firstborn daughter into bed when the ball game is on and try to hustle through the bedtime routine. If you dare leave one thing out ("But, Daddy, you forgot to kiss my blankie"), you'll hear about it for days.

Firstborns are creatures of habit. My buddy Moonhead, an only son with two older sisters, drinks coffee with a spoon in the coffee cup. Why does he do that? The spoon sort of gets in the way, doesn't it? But that's what Moonhead does. My firstborn wife doesn't like to have her back rubbed; she likes it scratched gently in an S shape. And the scratching has to start on her back *first, then* you can move to her arm or hand. It has to be in that order.

Achievers

Think *achiever* and Oprah Winfrey comes to mind. Her first attempt at acting in a movie, and what happens? She's nominated for an Academy Award for *The Color Purple.*

But this achiever's life has been far from easy. At age 9, she was raped by a family member and molested repeatedly throughout her childhood. She experienced the other triple whammy of a broken home, extreme poverty, and racism in Mississippi.

Oprah truly has come up from the bottom, and now she's flying. She has her picture on *O*—her own magazine—every month. She's the richest woman in all of America, and she's packed with personality plus. I've been at her studio four or five times. Every time, I have left believing that if she said to her audience, "Okay, ladies, we're going to run through that wall," they would do it. She has that kind of leadership potential. Whenever she announces her new book selection, someone should contact Amazon.com and the bookstores and clear floor space, because it will be needed. All Oprah needs to say is, "Here's my selection of the month," and the book becomes a bestseller.

Oprah is an achiever, a visual leader. She doesn't back down from the tough issues. Yet she also gives away a lot of money and prizes. People walk out of her studio feeling like they've been in the presence of greatness.

Pursuers of Excellence

Tiger Woods and Bill Cosby come to mind for me first. Both of these firstborns are known for pursuing excellence—for

setting the bar high, working hard to jump over it, and helping others jump over it too.

The Flip Side

Every day I sit back and marvel at how much the firstborns
in my life accomplish—and how well they do it.

But there's a flip side to all these wonderful talents that
firstborns have. Think of it this way. When I was a kid, there
was a little girl named Penelope, whose hand continually
shot up in class because she always had the right answer, and
the teacher always praised her in front of everyone. She had
to be a firstborn. As a kid, I always pictured many a misfor-
tune coming her way. I'm sure I felt the same as most of the
kids in that class, who referred to her as a "carrot-seeking
brownnoser."

Do others think the same about you?

Let's say you're on a committee at work. Your VP presents a
problem and puts it on the table for discussion. As a firstborn,
you can think circles around the middleborns and babies of
the family, so you quickly come to a conclusion—a conclusion
you're convinced is the right one and the only one. So while
all the others are still trying to form their thoughts, you jump
in with the solution. How do you think your co-workers are
going to feel? Will they be referring to you behind your back
as a "carrot-seeking brownnoser," or worse?

If you're married, do you lay down the law of what should
be done, and when—since, of course, you know best? Or do
you give your spouse some say in the plans, even if it takes
her longer to say? If you're the organizer of the family, do
you leave room for your husband (who might be a baby of

the family) and his surprises? Or is your schedule not flexible enough to accommodate him? Do you do all the work at home yourself because no one else will do it as well as you? How flexible are you in your relationships?

Recently a friend of mine was helping pack up gifts after a birthday party. Some of the gifts were breakable. Now, my friend is about as careful as a person can get, so there's no doubt about how cautiously she was packing the gifts. Yet she found herself in the midst of an exchange with another friend of the birthday girl, who saw things just a little differently. Here's the story in my friend's words:

> "You know," the other friend said, "you should pack the gifts this way, and then they won't break."
>
> I assured her I was being very careful and that they'd be fine.
>
> She frowned. "Well, you can remain in the dark and not learn anything . . . or you can listen to me and do it the right way."

Now, what birth order do you think the friend was? Come, now—is there *really* a right or wrong way to pack presents? To firstborns, yes, there is. To the rest of the world, as long as the presents arrive safely, what's the difference? Yet doing things "the right way"—her way—mattered more to that firstborn than her relationships with the women at the party.

Interesting, isn't it? Do you see why, because of your quick-thinking, perfectionistic nature as a firstborn, your relationships with others—whether at home, school, or work—can be problematic? But if you're aware of your tendencies, they don't have to be.

Traits of a Firstborn

Trait	Positive Aspects	Negative Aspects
Perfectionist	Does everything well	Overly critical and dissatisfied with his own performance
Driven	Ambitious, headed for success	Always under great pressure
Organized	Able to stay on top of everything	No room in life for flexibility
Scholarly	Able to think problems through and solve them	Sometimes thinks too much; is overly serious
List Maker	Gets things done; knows where he's going	Boxes himself in; becomes a slave to his list
Logical	Avoids pitfalls of compulsive behavior	Knows he's right, even when he isn't
Leader	Plays an important part in his family, community, etc.	Expected to do too much; always leaned on by others
Compliant	Known as a good guy	Known as an easy mark
Aggressive	Gets ahead in life; others look up to him	Tends to be selfish and to disregard the feelings of others

Pleaser or Controller?

There are two types of firstborns: the pleaser and the controller. Even though there are always exceptions to every rule, the two types of firstborns are fairly gender specific. The firstborn female tends to be the pleaser. The firstborn male tends to be the controller.

May I Help You?

If you're a pleaser, your motto in life is peace at any price. You bite off far more than you can chew. You're the type of person who would do anything for others while leaving nothing for yourself. You hold yourself responsible for other people's failures and negligence. Your goal in life is to make sure everyone is happy, because then, you reason, you count in life. So you run yourself ragged while trying to do favors for everyone else.

Because you bail folks out of messes, people like you. You're a nice person. You can always be counted on, and people seem to know your soft spots. You spend every day running on a tankful of guilt. You're driven by that guilt because you know you can never do enough. You just can't seem to say no.

There's nothing wrong with pleasing people. Let's face it: the world would be a much nicer place to live in if more people were bent on pleasing other people. But at what expense to *you* are you trying to please others?

If you're a pleaser and you work in a business, there will always be people who will say, "We'll just knock off an hour early and go play golf. She'll finish it."

If you're at home, you'll say, "I know he's supposed to do that, but I'll just take care of it."

If you're taking a class, you'll tell a colleague, "Sure, I'll copy those notes for you. Too bad you missed class."

My pleaser friend, I've got a word for you: *no*. I call it "vitamin N." And you need to start taking it by the boatload. If you find it hard to say no, simply say, "Let me think about that." (Don't make a spur-of-the-moment decision and add that activity to your Day-Timer.) Then, on the way home in your car, practice saying no numerous times in the car mirror when you stop at a light. By the time you get home, your mouth ought to be used to saying that word. Then simply make the phone call and say it: "No, I'm not able to help this time. But thanks for asking." Chances are, if you've always been the go-to person, there will be an amazed silence on the other end of the line. Your own jaw might drop at actually saying those words.

But you and those you love will be better off for it. And who knows? You might eventually have some time just for you.

Now there's a thought.

My Way or the Highway!

If you're a controller, you have a "my way or the highway" view of life. What you know is best, and it's the only way to fly. Your life philosophy is, "I only count in life when I'm in charge." And because you know what's best, you don't want to entertain anyone else's suggestions, since that would just be a waste of time.

If you're a controller, you already have the plan mapped out, even if you ask (as a token) for others' ideas. As a controller, you believe at the heart of it all that you're smarter than anyone else and can pull anything off (and oftentimes you can). But this kind of focus on things and getting the work done with little regard to relationships will come back to bite you. A company is formed by relationships—getting good people who can work together. And a family can't be run for long by a dictator. All family members need—and deserve—a say in "the plan."

If you're a controller, you have to remember that even if you're the top hog on the manure pile of life, you have to be sensitive to those who don't see life the same way you do.

If you're a firstborn, others are already in awe (or sometimes unnerved) by you, your ability to get things done, and your achievements. They see you as the supercharged Energizer Bunny. But the question is, what are you going to do with all the horsepower you have? How will you unleash it? With all that energy, you have to be careful and judicious, because you won't win in the long run by stepping on people. But you can win by coming alongside and empowering them. That's why you need to surround yourself with people of different birth orders, especially if you are a leader in business.

The really successful firstborns are the ones who learn how to make others feel important. Bill Cosby has a way of doing that. He and I were both invited by former governor Frank Keating and his lovely wife, Cathy, to perform and speak to over ten thousand people in an arena. In essence, I was Cosby's warm-up speaker. It was really neat, because I had Cosby all to myself for thirty-five minutes backstage, and just the two of us talked about life. I was impressed by his interest in what I thought about social issues, and his compassion for his fellow man came through loud and clear. Afterward I went away shaking my head, thinking, *What a wonderful time. That guy really made me feel important.*

Bill Cosby is doing it right. He's using his firstborn advantage to his advantage. But he's also using it for the advantage of others. He speaks about social and educational issues, particularly African American ones, from a passion to try to change the world for the better. He's taken a lot of heat for some of the things he's said. But isn't that true of any great firstborn leader?

4

Why Firstborns Are the Way They Are

> From day one, they're in charge. They always have the thickest photo album. They set the benchmark for every other child in the family.

Responded to voices in the womb. Walked at 6 months. Spoke in complete sentences before age 1. Perfected second language at age 2. Wrote name (first and last) at age 3. Learned instrument at age 4. Were a singing, knitting, and dancing prodigy at age 5. Babysat siblings at age 6. Babysat neighbors at age 7. Inspiration for three photo albums by age 8. At age 9, you were told by adults, "You can be anything you want to be." At age 10, you announced to everyone that you intended to rule the world.

You are pretty, smart, talented, and wise beyond your years.

You love and are loved. You do everything and you do it well.

If this is your history, then you are a firstborn girl.[1]

Laura Carter, founder, First Born Girls Social Club

I'll never forget the lively time I had when I spoke to the First Born Girls Social Club in Virginia. They were just launching into their second year as a group, and they were an energetic audience. The women there were movers and shakers of their community. No, they weren't all CEOs, but they were all achievers. They shared the common mission "to discover, celebrate, and share the unique contribution of First Born Girls to the world." These women had committed to laugh together, share together, and learn about prioritizing together. They had all agreed there was a great need for firstborns to schedule their personal and fun time in their Day-Timers—or they knew it wouldn't happen. I was impressed.

You see, I know firstborns well. My sister, Sally, is one. She's the kind of person who straightens up the brochures in the bank lobby when she visits there. (Yes, I watched this. It really happened.) My wife, Sande, is one. She's the lovely lady you'll find dusting our dining room chandelier at 2 a.m., just because she noticed a spot. And then there's my assistant, Debbie. If it weren't for Debbie, I'd forget half my speaking engagements.

As a baby of the family, I know how much I need these women. As my wife said once, "No, I'm not always right. I just know better than you." Who can argue with that? She does know better.

From day one, firstborns are groomed for success. They don't have a lot of room in their lives for flexibility and spontaneity. And it all starts with them being the guinea pigs for Mom and Dad.

The Making of a Firstborn

Firstborns have a unique position in the family. They're the oldest or the only kid in a family, so they don't have any buffer between them and their parents. That means, in a two-parent home, they get a double shot of Mom and Dad, with no competition . . . until little Johnny comes along, at least. No wonder firstborns are the group who feels most comfortable navigating the adult world. They lived in the house before sibling rivalry started.

> From day one, firstborns are groomed for success.

They also get a hefty share of parental time. According to a recent birth order study by Brigham Young University, "Firstborn children get about 3,000 more hours of quality time with their parents between ages 4 and 13 than the next sibling gets when they pass through the same age range," says assistant professor Joseph Price.[2]

From the very beginning, the focus is on the firstborn. Your mom and dad painstakingly chronicled everything from your first smile (or was it gas?) to the first time you rolled over, to your first step, to your first words, to your first day of school. They even had time to read to you at bedtime and play with you. Almost all your feats were clapped over wildly and documented by snapshots, videos, and complete parent and grandparent attention, especially if you were the

75

How to Create a Firstborn

Focus only on your child.
Make your child the center of everything you do.
Overrecord and overdramatize every milestone—rolling over, sitting up, taking that first step.
Make a big deal out of simple achievements, like smiling without drooling.
Treat your child as the star of the show.

first grandchild in the family and your grandparents lived in close proximity.

Every time you did something, it was a big deal. Your photo albums were soon bursting with pictures, all categorized. (By the time the third child in your family was born, he or she was lucky to get a few pictures in a shoebox.)

And because things were a big deal, your parents tended to overrespond. They overdid the praise. "Oh, look. You went poo-poo." (By the time child three was toilet trained, all your mom yelled was, "Make sure you flush." By then your parents had figured out that going poo-poo is, after all, a natural thing.)

> Every time you did something, it was a big deal.

When you were 2 and drew your first picture with black ink on a piece of paper, it had marquis time on the fridge for weeks on end (even though it looked like a grasshopper that had an epileptic seizure). Because everything you did was exaggerated, you grew up thinking, *I am what I do. And whatever I do has to be great, because then I'm worth something.*

When you played your first piece on the piano ("Twinkle, Twinkle, Little Star"), your parents celebrated it as if you were a maestro. Three years later, when your sister did her own solo, your parents just sighed and said, "Remember when Samantha did that?"

As the firstborn, you unconsciously set the benchmark for what a child should or shouldn't be like. That's why your mom and dad were bamboozled when baby #2 came along and was so different from you. And why was that?

Think of your family as a stage. You, as a firstborn, are the star, and you've been on stage by yourself for quite a while. Then along comes a supporting actor or actress or two. When you're already firmly entrenched in your position as the star, is it likely that the supporting actor or actress can take over your role? Probably not. (Unless the very important variable of the critical eye comes into play, which we'll talk about in chapter 6.) So what does that supporting actor or actress do? They play a completely different role, because that's the only way they can find success and their own place in the family.

No wonder the firstborn and secondborn in a family are as different as day and night. Take, for instance, Jimmy and Billy Carter. Jimmy, the firstborn—serious, studious, over-achieving—eventually worked his way to the presidency of the United States. But his younger brother, Billy, was famous for his beer drinking, for his rude and off-the-cuff remarks, and for generally behaving as if he didn't have a serious bone in his body. Sadly, he died too young.

Firstborn Perks

Because you were the firstborn in a family, you had certain perks since day one. Even as a young child, you made up rules that your parents followed. And your parents were new (and dumb) enough to fall for rules like:

I'll drink only out of the red cup, not the blue cup.

Mommy has to cut the crusts off the bread before I can eat my sandwich.

Spaghetti sauce is not allowed to touch the spaghetti.

Every pillow and stuffed animal needs to be aligned around the outside of my bed before I can go to sleep.

I always get a drink of water at bedtime from the *kitchen* faucet. Water from the *bathroom* faucet is not acceptable.

As a firstborn, you developed a definite set of patterns about your life and how things should go. Your parents, being new parents and having just you to focus on, fell prey to attending to all those intricacies of your personality. If you have firstborn children now, you probably have a refined understanding of your own childhood and all those requests.

Having Mom and Dad's attention was sometimes a wonderful thing; other times it may have been overwhelming (especially if you had a critical-eyed parent, as we'll talk about in chapter 6). You were the child in the family who always got things new—new clothes, new toys, etc.—because you were the oldest.

Firstborn Challenges

But there were also challenges with being a firstborn.

When your little sister or brother came into the family, all of a sudden your parents, Grandma and Grandpa, and even strangers were saying things to you like, "Oh, you're the big brother now. Do you like your little sister?" Any firstborn in his right mind would answer after a while, "Of course I don't like her. She's interrupting the flow of things around here. And Mom and Dad don't have time for me anymore . . . unless it's to help them change diapers." All of a sudden, you as the older child may become the errand boy and diaper changer. It's a rather rude awakening to a child who has been the star on the family stage for a period of years.

> When a job had to be done around the house, who did Mom or Dad call for help?

Because you were set in your patterns, you were the most susceptible to anything negative going on in the family, because that experience disrupted the normal flow of your life and relationships. If your parents fought, you were the one most influenced by it because your role models in life were adults, your parents. Your siblings, on the other hand, were looking to you first and your reaction to what was going on.

On top of that, when a job had to be done around the house, who did Mom or Dad call for help? It certainly wasn't your youngest sister, who had a variety of skills—all aimed at the goal of getting herself out of work.

As your siblings appeared, suddenly you were in charge— and responsible for all the other ankle biters in the family. So what did you naturally think of life? *This is so unfair!*

Can you identify with any of the following statements?

Things All Firstborns Hear

"I don't care what *he* did—you're the oldest."

"Take your little brother with you."

79

"Couldn't you keep your little sister out of trouble?"

"What kind of example is that?"

"I expect a little more out of you, young man."

"When are you going to grow up?"

"He's littler than you. You should know better."

Things All Firstborns Say

"How come he never has to do anything?"

"You're not letting her go, are you?"

"You never let me go when I was her age."

"Why does he have to come with me? Can't he stay home?"

"If I did that, I'd be grounded for life."

"Mother, would you get her out of my room, please?"

If so, there is no doubt that you're a firstborn.

A Thankless Job

There are many dangerous and virtually thankless jobs in this world.

Like the police officer who risks his life every day simply because he believes that ordinary citizens have a right to be protected from criminals.

Or the firefighter who rushes into a blazing building without regard for his own safety, intent on saving the life of someone else.

Then there's the coal miner, who spends his days in a darkened world far below the earth's surface.

Such people have my admiration and my respect.

But I'll tell you something. Each of those people has nothing on the person with the toughest job in the family.

No, I'm not talking about Dad, although his job can be plenty tough at times. Nor am I talking about Mom, even though we know she's really the glue that keeps the family together.

The toughest job in the family, hands down, goes to the firstborn.

As a firstborn, you know from experience what I'm talking about. You've always lived your life in the limelight as the perfect example for everyone else. You know what it's like to live with that burning desire to conquer the world—or die trying. Why do you have that desire? Because you were often pushed too hard and asked to perform beyond your capabilities.

Who is the person who mows the lawn? The firstborn.

Who rakes the leaves in the fall? The firstborn.

Who serves as the built-in babysitter? The firstborn.

Who's expected to help Mom in the kitchen and wash dishes night after night? The firstborn.

Who has taken out the trash since he was little and still does it when he comes home from college? The firstborn.

In a typical family, the oldest always seems to get stuck with the hardest chores. He not only keeps them until he moves out on his own, but he experiences what every firstborn hates: the adding of more and more and more chores.

What happens when younger siblings come along? If John figures it's time for little brother Bobby to take over the job, he can dream on. It's not likely to happen. Once the chore is assigned, it's assigned for life. That may be because parents don't want to take the time to "train" someone else to do the job. But that's not fair. Little Bobby may be the youngest, but he can pick up the dog plops in the backyard and toss them over the fence into the neighbor's yard just as well as John can.

Is it any wonder, then, that firstborn adults tend to take on more work? They've been primed to do it.

Consider these two common scenes:

Scene 1

Firstborn Maggie sits at the dinner table and watches little Jake push his peas away.

"Yuck," he says. "Gross."

Mom sighs. "Okay, dear, you don't have to eat them if you don't want them."

Maggie doesn't say anything, but she's incredulous. She remembers sitting at the table for an hour before eating her peas.

Scene 2

Firstborn Kyle sits upright at his younger sister's dance recital just the way he's been taught. His littlest sister, Megan, is bored. She dumps crayons all over the bleachers, slides down on her belly, and starts to draw. Kyle looks at his mom. *What's she gonna do?* he wonders.

His mom isn't even paying attention.

Kyle remembers what it was always like for him, and nothing's changed: "Sit up straight." "Pay attention." "Support your sister." "Quit slouching."

It's no wonder that firstborns grow up to be superorganized, superachieving, pillar-of-the-community type people. They can't—or don't dare—be anyone else.

Great Expectations

Why are firstborns treated differently than later children? I think it has a lot to do with the fact that firstborns are not allowed to be children for very long.

Let's say you're 3 years old when your brother is born. All of a sudden your parents see you as such a big girl, especially because your brother is so tiny and so helpless.

Three more years go by, and you're practically seen as an adult, while your little brother is still seen as a baby. Many parents tend to view their firstborn children as older than they really are. They expect them to grow up too fast.

Parents also have a lot of other expectations for their firstborns. They expect them to set a good example for all the children who follow them. Firstborns are to be the smartest, the best behaved, the best-looking, the most conscientious, the strongest . . . need I go on? And with such expectations, is it a wonder that many firstborns fail to measure up to their parents' exacting standards?

Firstborns have internalized the standards they grew up with, and now those standards are neatly woven into the fabric of their lives as adults.

Firstborns are goal setters; they are well organized; they are the sort of people who know where they're going, how they'll get there, and how long it's going to take to get there.

> Firstborns are not allowed to be children for very long.

So what's wrong with that? Absolutely nothing. But the problem arises when firstborns feel they can never measure up to the expectations their parents set for them—and those unrealistic expectations follow them into their adult lives.

All firstborns are perfectionists. Perfectionism is woven into their very natures, as are the standards they've grown up with. But there's a difference between *perfectionism* and *discouraged perfectionism*. Which one are you? Take the "Which Kind of Perfectionist Are You?" quiz on page 85 to find out. Do it right now. I'll wait while you do.

Healthy Perfectionist or Discouraged Perfectionist?

What's the difference between the two? The healthy perfectionist (also known as a pursuer of excellence) is driven to do everything she does as well as it can possibly be done. She'll give you every ounce of her ability. And as long as she knows she's done that, she'll be satisfied with what she's accomplished.

The discouraged perfectionist is never satisfied with what he has done. No matter how good a job he's done, he always thinks he could have done better. He feels discouraged and considers himself a failure.

The artistic genius Leonardo da Vinci was a discouraged perfectionist. Here's how he felt about himself, in his own words: "I have offended God and mankind because my work didn't reach the quality it should have."[3] Surprising words from the man who gave the world the *Mona Lisa* and *The Last Supper*, among his other incredible works of art.

Look back at your answers to the quiz. If you answered a or b, you're most likely a discouraged perfectionist. If you answered c, you have a healthy sense of self-worth in your striving for perfection. Here's what the quiz reveals about discouraged perfectionists:

Which Kind of Perfectionist Are You?

1. You've been asked to look into the cost of new playground equipment and make a verbal presentation of your findings at the next meeting of the neighborhood association. You would:
   a. immediately be afraid you wouldn't get the report done in time for the meeting.
   b. start worrying about whether you'd be able to talk to the right people and get the right cost figures.
   c. feel proud of yourself for being recognized as someone who could handle the assignment, and immediately begin working on it.

2. If you stopped by your best friend's house for a cup of coffee and she said, "I'm sorry, but I'm just too busy to talk to you right now," you would:
   a. wonder what you had done to offend her.
   b. become angry and figure that her behavior showed what she *really* thought of you.
   c. tell her you understand (and mean it) and ask her to call you when she has time.

3. If you were fifteen minutes late for work, you would:
   a. figure that everyone saw you come in late and probably were all talking about you.
   b. march into the boss's office, confess your misdeed to him, and then work during your lunch hour to make up for the few minutes you missed.
   c. realize that everyone gets held up now and then and promise yourself that you'll try not to be late again.

4. If you were balancing your checkbook and were fifteen cents off, you would:
   a. spend hours balancing your checkbook, vowing that you won't stop until you find the missing fifteen cents.
   b. decide that fifteen cents isn't really worth worrying about, but then lie awake all night wondering where you made the mistake.
   c. decide that fifteen cents isn't worth worrying about, and then quit worrying.

Question 1: Discouraged perfectionists are world-class winners at beating themselves up. They anticipate their own disasters and failures. They're the ones who walk out of a test and say, "I failed." They're fearful of not measuring up and figure, *If I put myself down first, then nobody else has to.* They're their own worst enemies.

Question 2: Discouraged perfectionists are very good at reading between the lines and figuring out what people really mean. They are constantly being rejected and slighted.

Question 3: A favorite pastime of discouraged perfectionists is magnifying their mistakes and flaws.

Question 4: Discouraged perfectionists have a difficult time figuring out when to let go. They'll spend hours agonizing over and wrestling with the smallest problems because they want everything to be done right.

If you see yourself as a discouraged perfectionist, don't give up hope. And don't let your own and others' expectations drive you crazy. You can learn to deal with life's little inconsistencies and imperfections and keep smiling all the while.

The key is to first identify which perfectionistic games you're playing.

Which Games Are You Playing?

Perfectionistic firstborns tend to play all sorts of games with themselves, says Dr. Miriam Adderholdt-Elliott in her book *Perfectionism.*[4] Do you play any of these games?

Mood Swinging

Your mood always depends on your latest success or failure. If the boss liked your report, you're on top of the world. If he thought there was room for improvement, you're crushed and sitting at the bottom of a deep, dark pit.

The Numbers Game

You gauge your worth by the quantity rather than the quality of your achievements. The result can be that you don't do anything as well as you could, but you keep on rushing from project to project, trying to get enough things done to feel good about yourself.

Telescopic Thinking

When you're looking at things you need to do, you seem to be looking through a telescope, so those things appear to be much larger than they really are. Conversely, when looking at what you've already done, you turn the scope around so your accomplishments look positively tiny.

Focusing on the Future

You did well in something—so what? You don't have time to sit around and pat yourself on the back. You're already too busy worrying about what comes next.

Pining over the Past

When you're not worrying about the future, you're brooding about past failures, wondering why you didn't do better and playing the "if only" game. "If only I had studied harder . . ." "If only I had put a little more effort into that . . ."

Putting Your Goals First

You might have time for recreation later, once your goals are met. You might be able to spend time with your family, but right now you have to keep pushing ahead on this project.

Let's face it: there are always times when you have to set aside the fun and family time to get work done. But as a perfectionist, you do this constantly, going from task to task so you rarely have time for yourself or for others who are important in your life.

Getting It Right

"I'm going to keep doing this until I get it right." In other words, you do a report for work over and over and over, and it's never perfect enough. You spend hours in your garden to get it looking "just right," and it never is. Nothing could ever meet your own expectations.

All-or-Nothing Thinking

You're not satisfied unless you're the best at everything you do. You may be the captain of your community soccer team, be the first-chair flutist in the community band, win Teacher of the Year, keep your home immaculate, and have three wonderful children who are respected by everyone. But if Betty Swanson defeats you in the election for president of the local PTA, you feel like a total failure.

Do any of these games sound familiar to you? If so, give yourself 10 points for each game, and tally your score.

How did you do? Rate yourself according to the following point chart.

70–80 points: You're the poster child for a discouraged perfectionist.

50–60 points: You're still giving yourself ulcers—and you don't need to.

30–40 points: You're doing pretty well for a firstborn, but you can do even better.

10–20 points: Everyone plays one or two of these games.

0 points: Either you're from another planet or you're not telling the truth.

How are you doing in the area of perfectionism? Are you a pursuer of excellence, as are Tiger Woods, Bill Cosby, and so many other firstborns? Can you give whatever you're doing your best shot and just get it done? Or are you a discouraged perfectionist who spends her days entrenched in "I'm never good enough" thinking? Are you so cautious and analytical that you never dare to move ahead?

As a firstborn, you are born and bred for perfectionism. Because you grew up with high standards and have internalized those standards, they are now woven into the fabric of your life as an adult. And you've even projected those high standards onto every person you come into contact with—whether you are conscious of doing it or not. That means that at home, at work, at your night class, at your daughter's school, with your friends over dinner, etc., the standards you were raised with live on.

But those standards don't have to hold you hostage anymore. The more you understand about birth order and how it affects you, the more you can use your firstborn character traits to your advantage. Keep reading.

5

Where Do I Go to Buy One of Those Firstborns?

You can't buy 'em, you can't teach 'em (at least not very well). A firstborn has innate skills that are hard to beat if he or she is balanced in life.

"There is definitely something unique about firstborns," says Laura Carter, founder of the First Born Girls Social Club. "We're not all extroverted. We're not all CEOs. But we all pursue high standards; we set high goals."[1]

I can sure attest to that. The firstborns in my life could clean my clock anytime. There's my firstborn daughter, Holly, who coordinates curriculum for grades K through 12 with amazing efficiency and calm. Just looking at the piles of books and papers makes me squirm. It would take me years to even get them sorted out enough to start the process.

There's my firstborn wife, Sande, who just knows how things ought to be run. And they're run with precision, flair, and artistic beauty in our house—the same way she ran her antique store, Shabby Hattie.

There's my son, Kevin, who juggles more creative writing and directing projects than I could imagine, all the while managing a busy career in the limelight of show biz.

There's my little friend Kayla, who, at age 8, organizes her mother's spice cabinet, plays a Vivaldi concerto on the violin, composes her own Irish dance on the piano, and is already thirty pages into *Moby Dick*—all within the space of two hours.

And during those same two hours, there I am with my feet up, once again enjoying *The Three Amigos*. (Not that there's anything wrong with that movie. It's my favorite of all time.)

See what I mean?

Firstborns are the organizers, the planners, the achievers, the ones who get to the top of the heap, no matter what heap they're on. They're recognized for their leadership ability in whatever circles they run in. In fact, it's impossible to hide that ability.

That makes firstborns unique. You stand out from the pack.

That's how the First Born Girls Social Club came to be. Laura Carter and her friend Gloria used to get together for lunch. They jokingly called the gathering "the meeting of the firstborn girls," since both were firstborns. A couple of years later, another woman, Jeanne, mentioned that she too was a firstborn girl (who had a firstborn daughter and a firstborn granddaughter) and would like to come to the sessions. So

Laura and Gloria decided to have some fun. They'd pretend they were part of a professional firstborn girls club and would "interview" Jeanne. Here were the questions they sent her via email:

1. When did you first know you were different?
2. What are your first memories of exhibiting First Born G [Girl] behavior?
3. How would your childhood friends describe you?
4. What is the birth order of your spouse?
5. How would you describe yourself?
6. What drives you?
7. How have you nurtured your First Born Girl and First Born Granddaughter?
8. What support do you need from other First Born Gs?
9. How can you contribute to the First Born G meetings?[2]

And that was the start of the First Born Girls Social Club. Who are the firstborn girls? They are, according to Laura:

Feisty
Independent
Rebellious
Smart
Talented

Bossy
Organized
Resilient
Nurturing

Gorgeous

Individualistic

Responsible

Leaders

Sassy

Creative

Loving

Understanding

Brilliant[3]

What's so special about the club? It's a place for firstborn girls and women to explore how being a firstborn contributes to their lives. Laura says:

> The first session was like a meeting of perfectionists anonymous, so that was our first discussion point. We all realized we had to lighten up. Many of us were working full-time or part-time or were stay-at-home moms, caring for children and aging parents. We all led extremely busy lives. Unless we scheduled free time for ourselves, we knew it wouldn't happen. There had to be some value to fun for it to draw a firstborn. Otherwise it was just another responsibility or something else to put on the calendar.[4]

So they began scheduling game nights. Members of the club will put them on their calendar. There's no "bring a dish to share" or "bring a beverage." They just show up. There's only a minimal fee of five bucks to cover the cost of snacks and beverages and fun prizes. Since firstborns' lives are filled with responsibility, the club is a chance to kick back, discuss, laugh, and just enjoy life.

The club plans two fun trips a year, such as a road trip to Savannah. "Firstborns will always be firstborns," Laura says. "You're not going to find anyone singing '99 Bottles of Beer' on the road trip. There are too many things to do. Two members wrote their business plans on the way to Savannah. One knitted her Christmas gifts."

And that's just for starters. The club also has an annual convention, and Laura has created a newsletter that features a famous firstborn every month, plus other intriguing articles, such as "Are You Productive—or Just Busy?"[5] Discussions focus on hot issues common to firstborns, such as time management, stress management, and prioritizing. "Everyone understands the pressure firstborns feel—the pressure to be perfect," Laura says.[6]

> Here's a good way to drive yourself totally bonkers: don't settle for anything less than perfection in whatever you do.

Ah, Perfection . . .

Here's a good way to drive yourself totally bonkers: don't settle for anything less than perfection in whatever you do. If you sing in the choir, make sure your voice is the clearest, purest, and loudest, and that you have all the important solos.

If you're painting a picture, make sure it's at least on par with anything Rembrandt ever did.

In bowling, never settle for anything less than a 300 game. Golf? You always have to shoot an 18.

I know what you're thinking: *Dr. Leman, you're being ridiculous. All the solos? Rembrandt? A 300 game is a once-in-*

a-lifetime feat for the best of bowlers. And shooting 18 holes-in-one in a row? No one could ever do that.

Exactly. But you see, that's perfection, and that's the sort of life many firstborns expect to lead.

Now, I've seen many excellent rounds of golf, but I've never seen one that was perfect. I've seen some beautiful paintings, but I can almost always find at least a tiny flaw if I look hard enough. And I know some people who are delightful, intelligent, artistic, and sensitive, but I've never known any who were perfect. In fact, in all of human history, there's been only one man who was perfect. So why are you expecting to be perfect yourself?

> Life is not a gymnastics meet, where five judges are holding up scorecards to evaluate everything you do. You don't have to run through life racking up a perfect 10 in everything.

Life is not a gymnastics meet, where five judges are holding up scorecards to evaluate everything you do. You don't have to run through life racking up a perfect 10 in everything.

If you go to Safeway with no eyeliner on, the clerks and customers aren't going to go running out of the store screaming. Neither are your mistakes written up in the daily newspaper, the way they'd be if you were a professional baseball player or the president of the United States. The only one who is judging you is *you*.

What does it mean to strive for excellence instead of perfection? Striving for excellence is reaching toward a goal that's attainable and not stopping until you get there. It's deciding, *I'm going to do things as well as I possibly can.* Excellence is within reach.

Think about It . . .

If 10 firstborn children were stranded on an isolated island, what would they be doing?
   a. hanging out on the beach, sunning themselves
   b. strategizing how to build a boat
   c. drinking coconut milk and doing karaoke
   d. selling plans to make sand castles
If you said b or d, you'd be right. If you said a or c, oops—some babies of the family must have been stranded on the island too.

Perfection is out of reach. "It's like the club member who couldn't leave the campfire until her marshmallow was perfectly roasted," Laura Carter says. "All the rest of us were on our second s'more. Dianne was still trying to make the perfect marshmallow. When we encouraged her to join us, she said, 'I can't yet. It's not perfectly done.' We all laughed because we could relate. We get it. And it's a relief to have that struggle out in the open."[7]

Ever seen that commercial for VISA, in which customers are paying for their purchases with their VISA cards and the world is happily humming along at the speed of light? Then suddenly someone pays with cash. Everything screeches to an abrupt halt. Everyone stares. And the poor guy paying with cash looks like a deer caught in the headlights of a car. That's what a perfectionist feels like when he fails—as if all of life stops (in fact, life is over), and everyone is watching his failure.

One minor thing can blow a perfectionist out of commission, and then he's stymied. He might throw a fit (an adult temper tantrum) or point the finger at someone else

Are You Chasing Perfection or Pursuing Excellence?

8 Ways to Know

1. The person chasing perfection reaches for impossible goals. The person pursuing excellence enjoys meeting high standards that are within reach.
2. The person chasing perfection bases self-worth on accomplishments. The person pursuing excellence values herself simply because of who she is.
3. The person chasing perfection is easily crushed by disappointment and is prone to throwing up his hands in surrender. The person pursuing excellence may be disappointed and hurt, but he doesn't let setbacks keep him from moving toward his goals.
4. The person chasing perfection sees failure as the enemy and is devastated by it. The person pursuing excellence seeks to learn from her failures so she'll be able to do better in the future.
5. The person chasing perfection remembers and dwells on his mistakes, and he thinks everyone else remembers them too. The person pursuing excellence will do his best to correct his mistakes and learn from them. Then he'll forget they ever occurred.
6. The person chasing perfection wants to be number one in everything and is happy only at the top. The person pursuing excellence is happy as long as she knows she has tried as hard as she can.
7. The person chasing perfection hates criticism and will go out of his way to avoid it. The person pursuing excellence may not always enjoy hearing criticism, but he will welcome the opportunity to improve his skills.
8. The person chasing perfection believes that winning is extremely important and has to win to maintain a healthy self-esteem. The person pursuing excellence can finish second and maintain her healthy self-image.

("It's *his* fault!"). When someone pursues excellence and life knocks him down, he gets up and gets going. He evaluates that failure, then uses it as a stepping-stone to figure out what he's going to do next. And after all, isn't that what life is all about—getting smarter for the next round?

A perfectionist spends all of her energy defending her position, right or wrong. She gets nothing done. The pursuer of excellence says, "Hey, listen, I welcome your input." No one likes criticism. But it's the smart firstborn who realizes that constructive criticism will help her grow and will help her hone her skills. That's why firstborns who pursue excellence gather people around them whom they can trust to give the whole skinny—not just a rubber stamp of approval. That's why firstborns need middleborns and babies of the family. All birth orders look at the world through different eyes.

It's the perfectionist who moans about the high-jump bar she has to go over. "It's so high. I'm never going to make it. I'll never meet that goal." It's the pursuer of excellence who says, "Okay, how high do I have to jump? How many tries do I get?"

The perfectionist is stuck in the past, in what she has accomplished before. The pursuer of excellence is moving forward. Her goals are in sight and are attainable.

The perfectionist often has the feeling that if she can't be perfect, she won't even try. The pursuer of excellence is a risk taker who says, "Well, I may not do this well, but I'm going to give it my best shot." The pursuer of excellence is the person who is constantly getting better, constantly growing, and always enjoying life. Don't miss out on the wonderful opportunities that life has to offer because of perfectionism.

What Are You Responsible For?

The relationships you enter into
The way you spend your time
The way you treat your body
What you put into your mind (books you read, movies you see, etc.)
The way you treat others
Your own happiness

What Are You Not Responsible For?

Your spouse's, roommate's, or child's bad day
The rain that spoiled your friend's plans for the day
The fact that your neighbor's babysitter is unavailable
The unexpected traffic jam that made you late for your appointment
The way others treat you and think of you
Anyone else's happiness

But It's My Responsibility . . . or Is It?

Firstborns are masters at feeling responsible for what other people say and do. Perhaps it's because you are taught so early in life that you are role models. Others are always watching you and patterning their lives after you, so, by George, you had better toe that old line for all it's worth.

Let me be clear. As a firstborn, you will tend to have a high level of responsibility. But you need to realize what is your responsibility and what is not.

If your spouse has had a hard day at work and comes home grouchy, it's not your fault. You can sympathize or give a back rub, but you must not pin the blame on your own shoulders. If he growls at you about anything and everything, you can tell him you're sorry he had a bad day and you'll do what you can to help him feel better, but you're not about to let him turn you into a scapegoat because his sales are down or his boss yelled at him. Stand up, be tough, and don't yield.

If your next-door neighbor wants you to babysit for her while she runs out to the store, but you're tied up and can't do it, it's not your fault. If she becomes angry, that's too bad, but don't let that make you feel guilty.

Children are especially adept at making their parents feel guilty. Let's say that at 10 a.m., you get a phone call from school. "Mom," your daughter says, "I forgot my math book. Can you bring it to school?"

Talk about bad timing. You have laundry going, and you're plowing full force into year-end accounts for your home business. And you have checks that have to go into the mail by 11 a.m. So what are you going to do?

The fact is, Melissa is 14, and she ought to keep better track of her math book. This isn't the first time she hasn't organized herself in the morning. Is it your fault she forgot it? Despite the whining and complaining you'll hear, you're smart to say, "Sorry, I can't bring it this morning. You'll just have to make do without it."

Think your daughter is likely to forget her book again? Especially when it means her math teacher says something about her responsibility level in front of the class?

Your daughter may be angry at you when she gets home, but when the red haze clears from her vision and you're still standing firm, she'll figure out quickly who's responsible for the math book. And it'll miraculously make its way into her book bag in the morning.

Suppose you have a co-worker whose personal life is always in an uproar. Not only is he always unloading his emotional stories on you, but he's falling behind on the job and calling

What Are You Busy Doing?

Jot down the answers to these questions:

> When are you happiest?
> What are your long-range goals?
> What are some things you do that you really don't want to (but you
>   do them because others expect you to)?

Is it possible that you're so busy being what everyone else wants you to be that you've never really given any thought to what you want out of life? If so, start giving it some thought now.

on you to help him get caught up. He's the sort of person who makes you feel guilty and responsible for his problems, even though you really have nothing to do with them. So what are you going to do? Continue to let him dump on you because you're a "nice person"? Or are you going to get tough and tell him that you can't pick up the slack for him and still do your own job?

He may get angry and he may bellyache, but that's not your problem. You aren't responsible, and you must not allow yourself to be taken advantage of in that way.

Sometimes you'll do things that others won't like. You are not responsible for their happiness. You can do your best to be sensitive to the needs and desires of others, but remember that some people will not be happy no matter how much you do for them. They will always ask you for more, more, more, and when you give it to them, they'll become even more demanding. There's a big difference between offering a helping hand and feeling responsible for other people's problems.

3 Winning Ways to Be Balanced in Life

1. Don't worry too much about what others think of you. You don't have to be the most successful, the best-looking, or the smartest person in the room. The only people worth knowing are those who like and respect you for who you are. If people admire you only because you're the best-looking or the most successful, they're pretty shallow—and they're making a pretty shallow assessment of you. Are those really the people you want as your friends?

2. Learn to laugh at your mistakes. Don't take yourself so seriously. Every human being makes mistakes. When you goof up, smile (even if it's forced at first). After a while, you'll find that failure isn't as scary as you once thought it was. And look at the flip side. Everyone sees you as perfect, but when you goof up, you might be setting them free from thinking they have to be perfect. When you think about your mistakes in that light, it makes them easier to take.

3. Remember your strengths. Don't sweat your weaknesses. Being a role model as a firstborn is sometimes hard to swallow, but so are a lot of things that are good for you—like spinach and broccoli. But because you've had high standards since you were a child, you've developed your natural skills and abilities far more than you would have if you'd just coasted along because no one expected anything of you. Celebrate how far you've come.

Does that mean you give everyone around you a kick in the pants and tell them to stay out of your life? No, that's not what I'm saying. You need people around you who can give you advice. But you can't let anyone *control* you.

Ultimately, no one is responsible for your life—including your happiness and well-being—but *you*.

Focus on Firstborns

Mara

She considered herself "just a mom," but she wanted to do something to influence her community in some way. So she contacted her local community center, which is twenty minutes from her home. Now every Thursday she and her two children, both under the age of 8, pack up snacks and juice and travel to the center to share them with the underprivileged children there. They also read books to the children while they await the arrival of their working parents. "It has become our favorite day of the week," Mara says. "It opened our eyes to what it was like to live a simpler lifestyle. Now every time I rush around preparing dinner, I think of those children who have so little. It has changed my perspective. My children often mention them too. It brings a healthy balance to our lives."

Andrea

This lawyer was married for four years before she realized how much she was breaking her husband's heart. "I was very successful in my career," Andrea says, "but I had no idea how much I was hurting the person I loved the most. I was stunned when he told me how lonely and ignored he felt." So she took action. Instead of filling her calendar with appointments every day, she blocked out lunch every Monday and took off Friday afternoons. And she said no to any cases that would have required her to work on the weekends. "I brought in less money for our family," she says, "but the change in our relationship was well worth it."

continued—

Nathan

Because of his demanding job as an architect and all the desk time and long hours it required, Nathan was struggling with being overweight—until he came up with a plan. He suggested that the office staff do their brainstorming session during the last half of their lunch break in the gym at the sports club next door. All his co-workers tended to eat lunch at their desks to get their work done anyway.

It's been a year since they started their basketball lunch sessions. The eight co-workers have dropped a total of forty-five pounds, and their brainpower has improved too. "More problems get solved there than at any other time during the weekday," Nathan says. Now there's a creative solution.

Jan

She was single and midforties, so she spent long hours at work every day, picking up the pieces from projects her co-workers couldn't finish. "One day it hit me," Jan says. "I had no life other than work. So I decided to do something about it." After that day, she began saying no to projects that would make her work overtime on Wednesdays and Fridays. "I knew suddenly trying to quit overworking would never work—for me or my boss—so I decided to change gradually."

Jan decided that Fridays would be her kick-back night but that she would start a reading/knitting night at her condo on Wednesdays. When she put a notice on the mailbox, she was surprised when three of her neighbors showed up. The group has had some wonderful discussions as well. Even better, one of the ladies loves to make snacks and always makes cookies. So all firstborn Jan has to do is open her door.

Brad

"I had a hard time making the transition from work to home," Brad admits. "I was so tense that I wasn't really being fair to my wife and kids." So he came up with an idea. He would call his wife every night when he was leaving work so she'd expect him home forty-five minutes later. It took him only fifteen minutes to get home, but on the way he would stop by the local Starbucks, sip a mocha latte, relax, and process for half an hour in order to clear his mind of work, and then drive home.

continued—

"That has completely revolutionized our family's life," Brad says. "It hit me how much our life has changed when my 4-year-old told me last night, 'Daddy, I'm so glad you like us now.'"

Jason
"I always wanted the perfect life—you know, a wife, white picket fence, two kids, a dog," Jason says. "But that never happened for me. I spent years blaming my parents for being bad role models and splitting up when I was 13. Then one day it hit me: it was my choice whether to move on or not."

And move on Jason did. He decided to stop focusing on himself and to pursue his dreams. He really wanted to influence children, so he became a Big Brother for 9-year-old Alex. For three years he spent Saturdays taking Alex to baseball games, concerts, and rock museums (rock collecting was a hobby of Alex's). They skateboarded and played football.

"It was like having my own kid. I loved it," Jason says.

Interestingly, while pursuing his dreams, Jason recently met a Big Sister, Maddie, who feels the same way about helping underprivileged children. . . .

It's All about Balance

"Balance is very important for a firstborn," Laura Carter says. "We feel so responsible for everything we do—and everything that we feel we should be doing. Delegating is difficult for a firstborn because she knows that she could probably do it better. So it's hard to let go."[8]

Is it hard for you to let go? Is that why you're overworked, overscheduled, and overstressed?

If so, now is the time to take some scissors to your schedule. What tasks could others do that you are currently doing? What tasks simply don't need to get done? And have you scheduled any time for yourself in the midst of whirling demands and activities?

Laura says:

Whenever I'm asked to do something, I've found it beneficial to say to myself, Laura, stop. Think. You don't have to make a decision today. Let's see what happens in the next couple of days. I consciously try to stop making immediate decisions. Because as a firstborn, I know if I make an immediate decision, I'll say yes. Firstborns have trouble saying no. So we practice saying as a group, "Not right now. Not yet." Both of those phrases don't make us feel guilty for saying no, but they keep us from saying yes so we can think about it first.[9]

What about firstborn men? Laura laughs. "They have a much easier time saying no because they're not as relational as women. They're not tugged in as many directions," she says.

Perhaps that's why firstborn women struggle the most with balance in their lives. "That's why there's a great need for firstborn women to schedule their personal time," Laura says. "An article I read once said that friendships with other women lead to longevity. But when we firstborns get busy, the first thing that goes is time with friends. Yet that's what studies show relieves the stress the most in a woman's life. So we actually do ourselves harm when we don't have a social time."[10]

How are you doing in the area of balance? Are you still trying to attain perfection? Or are you striving for excellence in a balanced way? Learn to "settle" for excellence, and your life as a firstborn will be transformed.

6

Has the Critical Eye Turned on You?

If there's anything firstborns struggle with, it's criticism. Did you have a flaw picker as a parent? Are you a flaw picker? Here's how to turn that around—for your own and others' good.

H ave you ever:

- started a project and not finished it?
- thought your work wasn't good enough (i.e., when you were young you tore up a picture you drew because it wasn't good enough)?
- run consistently late for work or social engagements?
- found the one imperfection in an otherwise well-done project?
- received a compliment and not known what to do with it?

Then let me ask you: did you grow up with one or more flaw-picking parents? You know: the kind that can spot a mistake from fifty paces and always point out what you did wrong? If so, and you recognize yourself in any of the tendencies above, you may be stacking the deck against yourself without even knowing it. You don't need enemies; you have yourself.

Well, it's time for things to change—for your good. You're going to love this chapter.

You may have grown up with a parent or parents who were loving, affirming, and encouraging in all things. If so, you were blessed—and then some. Frankly, this chapter is not for you. But it might be for someone you love and care about. So why not give it a read and extract the parts that are helpful to you?

The critical eye is by far the most vital factor in whether you will succeed or fail in your life as a firstborn. That's why I've given this variable its own chapter, and I've placed it right before we talk about putting your firstborn advantage to use at home, at school, at work, and in your relationships.

So many firstborns grow up with critical-eyed parents, and that criticism stays with them for life. It imprints them with the ability to find and magnify flaws—their own as well as others'. That's why criticism is a firstborn's Achilles' heel. That's why so many firstborns are discouraged or defeated perfectionists who set themselves up to fail. As children, they learned they couldn't do anything perfectly enough for their perfectionistic parent, so why bother?

Do You Remember . . . ?

How many of you remember the following scenario happening in your home as you were growing up?

"Make your bed, will you?" your mom calls from where she's making breakfast in the kitchen.

So, like the dutiful firstborn you are, you make your bed. You do your very best job—smoothing the bedspread, adjusting the sides so they're even. You carefully place your stuffed animals on your bed so all your friends can be in one place to enjoy the view for the day. You do everything precisely, because, after all, you're a firstborn, and that's the way you like things done.

Your mom whizzes by your door. "Good, honey, I'm glad you made your bed. Great job." But then she whisks in and fluffs your pillows a bit more and evens out the bedspread a bit.

What does this action say to you, the firstborn? *I can never do it right. I'm never good enough, never perfect enough.*

> I can never do it right. I'm never good enough, never perfect enough.

So what's your response, after enough of these subtle little messages from your parent (as well meaning as that parent may be)?

Some of you will dig in, hunker down, and try harder to please that parent.

Others of you will think, *Well, I might as well give up trying. I'll just let her do it herself.* And so you give up. Is it any surprise that, within a year or two, your bedroom is a mess and you rebelled against cleaning it? You *knew* you couldn't do it well enough to please your mom, so why bother trying?

Or how about this scenario?

Your dad asks you to clean out the garage so the two of you can use it for woodworking, your new shared hobby. One Saturday he has to work at his office, so you decide that's the

111

day. You get up early, determined to have it clean by the time he gets home so you can surprise him. You figure out where to store assorted items and even talk your mom into going to Wal-Mart to buy some bins for all the stuff that has collected in the garage. You're so knee-deep in clutter that you don't even think about lunch until 4 p.m. At 5 p.m., you stand up, feeling satisfied and exhausted. The garage looks incredibly different. You're proud of yourself.

You hear the garage door go up. Dad's home.

Smiling, you await his inspection. He drives in the garage, gets out of the car, and gives the garage the once-over. "Much improved," he says, nodding. Then he does the white-glove test on the window ledges. "But you still need to clean out the spiderwebs on the window sill. Guess you forgot that, huh?" And with that, he sweeps into the kitchen.

How do you feel? Deflated? Angry? Sad?

Now let me ask you: would you ever feel like doing anything to please your dad again? If you knew you couldn't gain your dad's favor, why would you bother? Your buddies don't care about a clean garage, and they're a lot more fun to be with.

Forget you, your eyes and your attitude say. And when it comes time for woodworking, you won't be readily available like you'd planned—on purpose. Since your busy dad doesn't pursue the project you'd planned together (he's an overachieving firstborn and is overly busy with work), it just dies in the water. Just like your relationship.

Evil or Clueless?

When you look back on your childhood, what do you think of first? Do you remember scenes like those just described?

When you stacked firewood but never did it right (at least according to your dad)? When you felt your mom's criticism and embarrassment when you misspelled one word in the school spelling bee?

I'm convinced some parents are downright evil. They're patterned after Cinderella's evil stepmother, who has a sharp and wicked tongue and who never tires of heaping abuse on her poor, fair-haired child.

I was in Kmart the other day, waiting for the blue light special to start (let's just say I like being economical), when a woman barged past me. She was obviously angry. In her shopping cart sat a little girl of perhaps 18 months, and the woman had a death grip on the wrist of a little boy who looked to be about 5.

> When you look back on your childhood, what do you think of first?

"I don't know why I bring you with me," she said, shaking his arm. "You never do anything but cause me trouble—"

"But, Mom," he whined. He seemed to be trying to stop the barrage coming his way.

"I don't know how you could be so stupid. That's what you are, stupid. Don't you have any brains at all?"

The little boy hung his head. I don't know what he had done, but my heart went out to him. Maybe he had knocked over a display or broken something. Maybe he had simply asked her for some candy or a toy after she had told him not to ask for anything. But whatever it was the little fellow had done, it wasn't worthy of the abuse his mother was heaping on him.

A little while later I saw the same family heading across the parking lot toward their car. This time the little boy let

113

go of his mother's hand and stepped off the curb when a car was driving down that aisle of the parking lot. There wasn't any danger involved, really. Anyone with a driver's license ought to be able to manage going around one small child in a large parking lot.

Once again the mom began screaming. "For crying out loud, Billy, watch what you're doing!" And then in a sarcastic voice she said, "Yeah, that's it. Go ahead. Run in front of a car now and get yourself killed. I guess that would be the end of my troubles, wouldn't it?"

She kept up her tirade all the way to their SUV. I couldn't hear what she was saying, but I could still hear the anger in her voice as she loaded her packages into the car, strapped the children into their car seats, and backed out of the parking space. I caught the little boy's dejected face in the back window.

I felt like running after them and yelling, "Stop! Stop! Don't you see what you're doing to your child?"

But of course I didn't. I know what I would have heard, as mad as that mama was. Things like "Who do you think you are?" and "It's none of your business anyway." And then things only would have gone worse for the boy. I did send up a prayer, though, to God Almighty, that this mother would begin to see what she was doing to her son.

Now, let me clarify. If the boy had done something deliberately wrong, he should have been disciplined. But discipline is correction that is done to change a behavior, not to humiliate or intimidate a child. It is done not in anger but with careful thought.

> Some parents are so frustrated with themselves and their life situations that they are angry all the time.

114

But some parents are so frustrated with themselves and their life situations that they are angry all the time. And where does their anger land? You guessed it: on the firstborn.

"You are so stupid."

"You dummy."

"What a klutz!"

"Can't you do anything right?"

"You're hopeless, do you know that? Hopeless!"

"You're the messiest kid I ever saw."

"Don't be such a little jerk."

"I'll be glad when you're gone. I need a break."

"If a bird had your brain, it would fly sideways."

> When a parent says to a child, "You're no good," the child believes her. *If Mommy says I'm no good, it must be true.*

Did your parents ever say these sorts of things to you? Have you ever said them to your children? The sad thing is, many parents have no idea how much their children love and respect them. Sadder yet, when a parent says to a child, "You're no good," the child believes her. *If Mommy says I'm no good, it must be true.*

Constructive, or Not?

Not all critical parents are like the woman in Kmart. Critical parents can also be as smooth as honey and just as sweet as they correct their children continually. They feel they have the child's best interest at heart—but what they're really pushing is their own agenda.

Here's a good example. You and your mom are over at an adult friend's house for lunch. As you eat, your mom peppers her conversation with her friend with these comments to you:

"Sit up straight, please."

"Don't slurp your soup."

"No elbows on the table, please."

How do you feel after that experience? Any child—particularly a firstborn, who is very sensitive to criticism—would likely be thinking, *Like I want to go through that ever again. No thanks. Mom can go to lunch by herself. I'll pretend I'm sick so I can stay home.*

> So many well-meaning parents barrage their children with "constructive" criticism.

Yet so many well-meaning parents—moms especially, but dads aren't immune either—barrage their children with "constructive" criticism.

Is there anything wrong with constructive criticism? Not really, especially if the comments are true. If you, as a child, run off to school without combing your hair, you would need someone to tell you to get back in the bathroom and comb it. If you are slouching and shuffling, it's good that someone is concerned about your posture. But here's when the problem occurs: when children don't hear anything but a steady stream of criticism.

Some parents are very quick to point out what their children are doing wrong, but they never open their mouths when they see their children doing something right. That's a mistake of major proportions. You ought to know, because you, as a firstborn, lived through a childhood of it.

No wonder you sometimes don't feel good enough or worthy enough.

The "Do It for You" Syndrome

Most firstborns have also fallen prey to parents who want to do everything for them. Here's what I mean.

Bruce has a project due at school, and he wants to do the best job he can. (He is, after all, a firstborn.) His class is studying Eskimos and how they live, so he makes an igloo out of sugar cubes, cuts a few whales out of construction paper, and fastens the whole thing to the inside of a shoebox. The problem is that the igloo looks like prime property for urban renewal, and the whales look more like Thanksgiving turkeys.

Bruce wants to show Mom his handiwork, and he stands there looking as proud as the proverbial peacock as she sees what he's done.

> **Did You Ever Hear . . . ?**
>
> "Quit slouching."
> "Come on, you can tie your shoes better than that."
> "Did you even try to comb your hair this morning?"
> "Stop shuffling your feet."
> "Sit up at the table."
> "What are you, stupid?"
> "_____"
> [fill in the blank]

She resists the urge to say, "What are those turkeys doing swimming in the Arctic Ocean?" Instead, having read all the parenting books and knowing she's not supposed to be "negative" with her children, she tells him he's done a terrific job and sends him out to play. As soon as he's out the door, she starts pulling the entire thing apart and doing it over.

117

But Bruce is no dummy. He notices later that substantial improvements have been made on his original effort. He may be only 8, but he realizes what this means: his own effort wasn't good enough. That sends an unfortunate message to the child, and it may be a long time before Bruce is able to take pride in anything he does.

Or picture little Jessie sitting at the table with her family, trying to cut her meat for the very first time. Daddy is about to have a stroke watching her because she is so slow and unsure of herself.

First of all, she holds the knife upside down.

"No, honey, it goes the other way."

"This way?"

"Yes, that's good, but . . ."

Now she's put her knife in front of the fork instead of behind it, with the result that the meat is jumping around on her plate as she tries to cut through it. She makes a violent sawing motion and almost knocks over her milk.

Her firstborn, perfectionistic dad has had enough, so he grabs her plate. "Here, I'll cut it for you."

"But, Daddy, I want to do it."

"I've been watching you, and you can't do it," he says. "At the rate you're going, you'll still be here next Thursday. Let me have it. I'll do it for you."

It's too bad that Jessie's father didn't have enough patience to let his daughter cut her meat for herself, and that Bruce's mother didn't realize it was her son's best effort that counted. Both of them, by their actions, sent a message that said, "You're not good enough on your own. You're always going to need someone to bail you out."

Later on in Jessie's life, her father will probably be doing her school science project for her, and when Bruce gets a paper route, his mother will probably get up every morning to help him fold and deliver his papers.

If you told either one of those parents that this sort of behavior is actually critical of their children and harmful, what do you think they'd do? Their jaws would drop, and they'd think, frankly, that I was smoking something that was making me loopy. But the truth is, such behavior *is* critical. Those parents aren't allowing their children to grow, to become self-sufficient, and to feel good about themselves. Later on in life their children will know that everything they do is doomed to failure, and they'll always be looking for someone to bail them out.

> "At the rate you're going, you'll still be here next Thursday. Let me have it. I'll do it for you."

Do you remember such scenes happening in your home? How did you feel about them then? How do you think they're influencing your thoughts about yourself—and your actions—now?

Don't Worry, I'll Make Up Your Mind for You

When firstborn Lorraine came to see me for counseling, she was full of anger toward her parents. She also had little self-worth. Yet when we began talking, all she could remember of her childhood were blue skies and sunny days.

This twentysomething had had two years of piano lessons, had become proficient in ballet and gymnastics, and had gone to an exclusive camp every summer. The family lived in a pleasant neighborhood, and Lorraine always had the best of everything. Her parents even helped her get accepted into one of the finest colleges in the country, and despite the fact that they were not wealthy by any means, they helped pay for her education there. Lorraine had always had everything she could need or want, so why was she so unsure of herself? Why was she so angry with her parents?

When we began to look at things a little closer, an interesting pattern began to emerge.

"Did you really want to take those piano lessons?" I asked Lorraine.

"No," she said, "but it was important to my mother that I learn to play the piano. When I finally convinced her, after two years, to let me stop taking the lessons, I know she was really disappointed."

"And the ballet?"

"I remember crying the first day of ballet class. I hated it—at least at first."

"But your mother . . ."

"Oh, yeah, she insisted."

It turned out that even the college she went to was her father's alma mater. What had Lorraine always been interested in? Pursuing a degree from an art school. But her father wanted her to be successful in the business world, so that's why she had a degree in business administration.

Lorraine's parents, you see, always wanted what was "best" for their daughter. The catch is, evidently they felt only *they* knew what was best. Lorraine didn't have any say in her own life.

Not only that, but whenever she didn't come through as they hoped she would, they were disappointed in her. She could see that. Oh, they never told her they were disappointed, but they showed it in plenty of other little ways. When she quit taking piano lessons, her mother's sad expressions, sighs, and body language toward her daughter did as much damage as if she'd just said to the girl, "I think you're a real dummy for not learning how to play the piano. Look at the opportunities I'm giving you. And what are you doing with them? Nothing."

Lorraine got the message. She was letting her mother and father down, but they were really too nice to say anything about it.

So what did her subconscious say about it? *Poor, long-suffering Mom and Dad. Trying to be so nice to me when I keep disappointing them.*

It took awhile, but eventually Lorraine realized that although her parents had never yelled, called her names, abused her verbally, or told her they were disappointed in her, they had indeed been critical of her. And now that she had finished college, she realized she was carrying on where they had left off—second-guessing her every step, questioning her abilities, putting herself down. She also had an extremely difficult time making up her mind about anything and always looked for someone else to choose for her.

Once she realized her self-doubts had grown from the way her parents had always dealt with her, Lorraine was ready to make an attempt to be gentler with herself. She began to

> Lorraine's parents always wanted what was "best" for their daughter. The catch is, evidently they felt only *they* knew what was best. Lorraine didn't have any say in her own life.

think, for the first time, about what she really wanted out of life. And guess what? If what she wanted out of life didn't line up 100 percent with what her parents wanted for her, oh well. It shouldn't stop her from moving ahead.

Was Lorraine's case unusual? Not at all. I've known dozens and dozens of men and women just like her—most of them firstborns—who were never able to grow into poised, self-confident adults because their parents wouldn't let them.

Why the Firstborn Gets It the Worst

Do any of the stories I've shared resonate with you and your experience growing up? Most often it's the firstborn—you—who locks horns with the critical parent. Why? Because more is expected of the firstborn. In fact, you as the firstborn are often treated as an adult, someone who should "know better" and "do better." But you are experiencing things for the first time—things the parent has done over and over and over—such as crawling, walking, running, navigating the kindergarten playground, taking a math test for the first time, cleaning your bedroom, and playing on the Little League team. Frankly, how *could* you do something better that you've never even done before? Much—too much—was expected of you.

You were the "experimental" child—the lab rat, if you will. Your parents, being new parents, were experimenting on you. They tried every trick from the stacks of books they read about child rearing. Some things worked; some didn't. And you got the brunt of all of it. By the time you were in junior high, your parents may have realized they were too harsh with you, so they determined to do better from now on. That's really good news for your 10-year-old sister, Megan, and your 7-year-old brother, Chase, but it doesn't do you any good. The mark of "discouraged perfectionist" has already been stamped on your personality with indelible ink.

So much has to do with the parent. Was one of your parents (or both) a flaw picker? Were they always "should-ing"? ("You *should* do this." "You *should* do that.")

A critical-eyed parent can defeat a firstborn. For example, if a family has two sons (or two daughters) and at least one critical parent, guess what's going to happen? The firstborn will become a slob and a procrastinator.

> You were the "experimental" child—the lab rat, if you will.

He'll be extremely sensitive to criticism because he feels like he doesn't measure up. The secondborn will overtake the firstborn—at the firstborn's expense.

Having a critical-eyed surgeon is a great plus. After all, if you were going under the knife, you'd want someone with an analytical, critical eye. But often the skills that help you succeed in the workplace will kill your relationships at home. A critical-eyed parent is deadly to a child's self-worth.

The Critical-Eyed Father

There is a very key relationship between a father and a daughter. And if the father is critical-eyed, it can greatly affect the firstborn daughter.

Let's say the family looks like this:

123

  Firstborn daughter
(six-year gap)

———

  Firstborn (and only) son
(three-year gap)
  Little Schnooky (baby girl)

Now add in these elements. The father has been extremely exacting of the firstborn daughter, making her toe the line in every way. She's become a goody-two-shoes who would never do anything wrong. She'd never think of violating any rules.

Along comes her brother. He's no problem because he's the first boy, so he's different.

But then along comes little sister. She's about as different from the firstborn as she can be. She's able to manipulate Dad like no other. Even more, Dad was the youngest in his family, so he identifies with Little Schnooky and overly protects her. And Little Schnooky knows it. She becomes highly skilled at using people—especially Dad—to her advantage.

So where does that leave the firstborn daughter? Out in the cold. Dad pays no attention to her—and when he does, it's always to criticize her. So is it any surprise that she steps back from her firstborn role and begins to break rules and walk to a completely different drummer than the rest of the family? She's a discouraged perfectionist. She can't do anything right anymore, so why bother? And I daresay that her relationship with her sister is not top priority in her thoughts (but murder might be).

A daughter's view of men and how she should be treated by them is formed by her father. How did your father treat you? How are your relationships with men today as a result? Did your younger sibling leapfrog over you as a firstborn and assume the firstborn role—at your expense—because of a critical-eyed father?

> How Daddy treated you as a daughter is a key issue that will influence you all your life.

How Daddy treated you as a daughter is a key issue that will influence you all your life. But it doesn't have to incapacitate you as an adult. In this chapter, we'll talk about ways to move on. You don't have to stay stuck in the past. A wonderful future and freedom beyond your imagination are awaiting you.

Great Expectations

Expectations are interesting, aren't they? Every parent, whether they admit it or not, projects expectations onto their children. Consider this common scene.

"Okay, kids. We're going to the grocery store. I only have to get a few things. Don't ask for any treats. I want you to behave yourselves. Keep your hands to yourselves and keep your mouths shut, and we'll get done fast. I have to rush home to cook dinner because your father has an appointment tonight."

The mother may think she's explaining things to the children, but what is she really saying? "Hey, kids. We're going to the store, and I expect you to misbehave."

So what do the kids do? What they've been expected to do: misbehave.

Those kind of negative projections are what you as a firstborn take forward into life, because Mom and Dad were always highlighting the negatives, not the positives. And that trained your naturally critical eye to work against yourself. No wonder it's easy for you to think negative thoughts. You've been trained to do that since your childhood.

You see, within each of you there is a camera, and that camera snaps a picture at key moments in life. I talk about this in my book *What Your Childhood Memories Say About You*.[1] Like the time you fell off your bike and scraped your knee. Or the time you were embarrassed in front of a group. There are certain events more than others that your brain remembers. Why? Because those events, pieced together, form your "private logic," a term coined by psychologist Alfred Adler. (We also talked a little about this term in chapter 2.) Your private logic is the way you see yourself; it's your view of life. It includes the way you seek attention or handle conflict. It's revealed through how you finish this sentence: "And the moral of my life's story is . . ." Your private logic tells you when you count in life, when you matter.

When Do You Count in Life?

When do *you* think you matter? Do you believe you only matter when:

    you dominate, control, and win?
    you avoid conflict and keep the peace?
    you keep everyone happy?
    you are the center of attention?
    you get your way?
    you're moving ahead to a goal?
    you meet your goal and line up the next one?
    you're contributing to others' well-being?
    _____? (fill in the blank)

Let My People Go!

Firstborns like to live life cautiously. They don't like surprises. (Oh, how I found that out when I planned a walloping surprise party for Sande, my firstborn wife, on her birthday . . . and she cried. I felt like such a loser. I went to college for thirteen years, and that's the best I could come up with? But it honestly never entered my baby-of-the-family brain that she wouldn't love a surprise. Ah, now I know better. . . .) Firstborns don't like curveballs. (I've also learned not to invite folks to dinner spontaneously.) They will try new things on their own timetable. But once they get that new thing down pat and get confident, watch out. They'll run over the middleborns and babies.

But the firstborn who is tied down by the weight of a critical-eyed parent will never be free to fly to his full potential until he decides he wants to be free.

Of course, in this day and age, it's in vogue to point your finger backward at your parents. "It's Mom's fault." "It's Dad's fault." Sure, your critical-eyed parent might have hammered you so hard that he or she conditioned you to see the negative. You were deprived of the encouragement that everyone needs, so no wonder you think of a glass of water as being half empty rather than half full. You felt you failed continually. You were put down so much that you finally decided not to try anymore because your parent would always find the flaw. Some of you even had *two* critical parents. Give yourself a pat on the back for surviving such an experience.

And you're right. Your parents shouldn't have done what they did. What happened to you shouldn't have happened to you. But where does all this retreading of the past get you?

Just angry and down in the dumps, wallowing over and over in the same pit. Is that really where you want to stay? What do you, as a firstborn who wants to succeed and who's born to be a mover and shaker of this world, have to gain from that?

If you realize what's in your background, evaluate how you responded to it then and how you respond now, and decide you want to move on from here, *then* you can get somewhere.

Academy Award–winning actor Gene Hackman had a big decision to make, and it had everything to do with his relationship with his father. One Saturday morning in 1943, when Gene was 13 years old and living in Danville, Illinois, he was at a friend's house, playing in the yard. He glanced up just as his father was driving by. His father waved, and in that moment, as he caught his father's eye and saw his parting wave, Gene knew his father was never coming back.[2]

There's no denying the hurt Gene's father caused him by walking out of his life. Yet over time, Gene had a greater deal of empathy for people's mistakes in life, and after confronting his father about leaving the family, he chose the way of grace.

"It was silly of me to expect him to change or to understand what he had done," Hackman said. "So I decided I wasn't obliged to be angry anymore."[3]

The fact is, we're all flawed and in need of grace. Your parents weren't perfect people. But they probably did the best they could with their resources, education, and circumstances. They most likely did what they thought was right. Now, you could debate whether their choices were right or wrong until the cows come home. Fact is, you and your parents were locked in a power struggle. It was all about winning—at any cost. And the more powerful your parent was, the more compelling his or her drive to win was. (More on that in chapter 7, where firstborn parent meets firstborn child head on.) So most often you probably ended up on the short end of the stick.

> Isn't it time for you to move on? Why are you choosing to remain in a power struggle with those who are no longer in authority over your life?

Let me ask you: isn't it time for you to move on? What's past is past. Now that you're an adult, why are you choosing to remain in a power struggle with those who are no longer in authority over your life? You can—and you need to—sidestep that power struggle. Say good-bye to it. If you don't, you'll be repeating the very same patterns with your own family.

But how do you start?

It's Time to Fight Back!

Life may have kicked you square in the teeth. There's no debating that. But ask yourself this: are you going to use that as an excuse for why you don't succeed in life? Are you going to wallow in how unjust life (or a certain person) is? Or are you going to suck it up and let your experience motivate you to overcome such adversity?

Damage inflicted by a critical parent can last a lifetime if you let it. You could be 90 years old and still react to things on the basis of how your parents treated you when you were a child. Or you could be 55 and still have to put up with a critical, picky parent who won't ever recognize that you're grown up and don't need to be treated like a child. Or you could be 23 and still living at home while you get yourself established in a career. That means you face the critical eye every day.

But guess what? It's never too late—or too early—to get free.

How can you do it?

Consider the Moment

Almost every parent, at one time or another, has lost her cool and said something like, "Don't you do anything around here but make messes?" or "All you do is cause me trouble."

That's because every parent is human. She's made out of flesh and blood, and she'll get to the boiling point and say things she doesn't really mean.

If you ever poured a bottle of syrup all over the carpet, your mom probably said quite a few of those things. It didn't mean that you really were the sloppiest kid in the world, or that she couldn't wait until you were grown up and gone, or any of those other things she probably said.

You may not have done anything. Your dad may have had a terribly stressful job that kept him jumpy and on edge, and this was reflected in the way he treated you.

Consider the moment in those instances.

You'd think that children would be smart enough to watch for the right moment to ask their parents for things, but I know from experience with my own kids that this just isn't so. It sometimes seems they pick the absolutely worst time to ask for something.

I may be crouched under the kitchen sink with a couple of wrenches, fighting a leaky pipe, when one of my children will come up and ask me if I have time for a quick game, or something or other. ("Does it *look* like it?" I want to say. But, of course, being the professional psychologist I am and knowing the impact this would have on my children, I don't.) But then, if I'm enjoying the rarity of a few days off and have some time to spare, no one seems to want to do a thing. That's just how life works.

When I was a youngster, my timing stunk too. How well I remember. I excelled at interrupting my dad and mom in the midst of projects that required their careful consideration. And today my kids do the same thing to me. Funny how that goes.

So consider that your timing in a particular event may not have been tuned very well to the mood and availability of Mom and Dad. Did that mean they were right in what they said? No, but they were human. Perhaps you should cut them—and yourself—some slack.

Is Your Parent Jealous?

What? My dad jealous of me? No way.

Are you sure?

Almost all parents will tell you that they want their children to have it better than they had it—and I suppose most of them think that's true. But deep down inside there may be some jealousy that erupts into a critical attitude.

Jimmy's father, for instance, is always saying how proud he will be when his son goes off to college. He'll be the first one in the family who's ever done that. But no matter how often he may say how proud he is, underneath it all he resents the fact that he had to drop out of school in tenth grade. Because of this, he does his best to keep Jimmy in his place. He keeps up a steady barrage of belittling comments, overlooking the good and emphasizing the bad.

Jimmy becomes frustrated and withdrawn, wondering why he can't do anything to please his father. He may grit his teeth and determine to try harder and harder and harder. But no matter what he does, it's never good enough—for his father or, eventually, for himself.

And then there's Judi's mother, who says she's proud of her daughter's beauty and popularity. Yet she can't find a decent thing to say about a single one of the boys her daughter has dated. She also finds things to nag Judi about, such as her long bangs, the new jeans she bought, and her once-a-month pudge.

Poor Judi soon becomes discouraged in her appearance. It never occurs to her that her mother, who is average-looking, is jealous.

Think I'm crazy? Jealousy is not as rare as you might think. I see it in counseling sessions on a regular basis. If your parents were supercritical of you, take another look at the situation. It could be that they were simply jealous.

Is Your Parent Critical of Everything?

Charlotte couldn't understand why her mother was always picking on her. She said, "I can't seem to do anything right. Nothing is ever good enough, and I suppose I'm just a real disappointment to her."

"Was your mother critical only of you, or critical of everything?" I asked.

She looked startled. "Well, she never really says an encouraging word to anyone."

"So she's always critical?"

"I asked her once how she was feeling," Charlotte said, "and I'll never ask again. She gave me a ten-minute lecture on everything that was wrong with her."

Firstborn Charlotte had a problem, all right, but it wasn't with herself. It was with her mother's approach to life.

What am I saying? Some people are impossible to please, and there's nothing you can do about it. They see all of life through dark-colored glasses.

What can you do if your parents are impossible-to-please people? Not much for them. No one will change them unless they're willing to work on changing themselves. So don't spend your time and energy trying to move an immovable wall.

But you can do something for yourself. Realize that your parents' treatment of you has nothing at all to do with you, your abilities, and your accomplishments. It may not be easy to learn to grin and bear it, but that's just about the only thing you can do. If you aren't living with your parents, you may want to carefully choose the times you interact with them. If you are living with them, either make plans to get your own place or limit your interactions by reorganizing your schedule. Let's be blunt: there are days when you can handle the criticism and negativity, and there are days when you can't. Only you know when those days are, so use that knowledge to your best advantage.

> Some people are impossible to please, and there's nothing you can do about it. They see all of life through dark-colored glasses.

Is Your Parent Disappointed in Himself/Herself or a Spouse?

If your parent is a chronic fault finder, he may not really be picking at you (even though it sure seems like it). He may be picking at himself—or his spouse.

Dad may be thinking, *Here I am, 40 years old and still in the same old job. I told myself I'd be a millionaire by the time I was 40, and instead I haven't done anything with my life.* So he comes home from work angry and frustrated and starts yelling at his daughter.

Who is he really mad at? Himself. But he can't pick at himself, so he finds a convenient substitute. And the firstborn child is always the first punching bag.

Or Mom is angry because she's had a fight with Dad. So when her firstborn son does something—anything—that reminds her of her husband, she goes on the attack.

The son is left wondering, *What did I do?* But he hasn't done anything at all—except get caught in the cross fire of his parents.

As you consider these reasons, my guess is that some of them will hit home. If you learn to recognize your parents' weaknesses and acknowledge that parenting is a painful process of trial and error (complete with baggage every person brings from his or her own past), you can see how parents can become critical-eyed. After all, they are living, breathing, thinking, feeling, and often damaged human beings—not machines.

Your parents may have read all the baby books they could get their hands on, but once you actually came into the picture, all that "wise" advice was about as useful as a snow shovel in the Sahara. So they learned the hard way—and they took it out on you, the firstborn.

Was what they did right? Many times, no. But can you change those actions now? Should you take your frustrations out on your siblings, who were treated better than you because Mom and Dad knew better later?

No to both questions. The only way for you to become free is to realize that your parents were human and to decide to forgive them so you can move on with your life. Otherwise your bitterness and anger will hold you back.

Does forgiveness mean you push all the bad aside and pretend that what your parents did (or didn't do) never happened? No. It means acknowledging what happened, including your parents' weaknesses and your own bias, and then choosing to step out of the chains of those memories—for good.

Making Peace with Your Parents

Is making peace easy? No, because it involves risk—opening your heart to people who have hurt you and changing your own attitudes, as Gene Hackman did toward his absentee father. The following steps are simple, but I urge you to try them. Many of my clients who have followed them have come back to me with smiles and joyful tears, saying, "Doc, it really, really works."

I'd like to see that same smile on your face. And there would be nothing that would bring me more joy than seeing you step out of the muck of the past and confidently into your future. You're a firstborn. You're born to fly like an eagle. But first you have to allow yourself to drop the chains that keep your feet locked to the fence post. So do it for your own sake.

Tell Your Parents How You Feel

If at all possible, gently and lovingly talk to your parents. Tell them about your experience and your feelings—not in a bitter, accusing way, but as factually as you can. Talking things out with them will help all of you, because chances are, they know they didn't always treat you right. They may feel as bad about things as you do, but it's hard for them to face up to it. (Who among us doesn't struggle to admit when we're wrong?)

It's also possible that your parents haven't the slightest idea you have those feelings of resentment, and they will want to do everything they can to make things right between you. They might even be feeling the distance or division between you but don't know what has caused it.

If they reject you or seem unwilling to even think about the possibility that they've made some mistakes, you'll at least have the satisfaction of knowing you tried to make things right—something especially important to a first-born, who has a strong concept of what's right and what's wrong. Don't you think that's much better than keeping your mouth shut for now but then later exploding from suppressed anger?

If what you have to say is too painful to tell them in person, put it in writing. Avoid being harsh, because it will put them on the defensive. Use phrases like "I felt _____ when X happened" instead of "You did X." Be firm, but be nice.

If your parents have died, or if your parents don't seem to care or refuse to listen to you, find someone else to talk to—a counselor or pastor—who can stand in your parents' place and help bring healing to the relationship. If your parents are still living, consider that you have tried. It is their loss, not yours. You have tried to do the right thing by them, and that's what you will remember.

Remind Yourself That It's Not Your Fault

Did you know it's not your fault that your parents didn't treat you as well as you wanted them to? Well, it's true.

Remind yourself of this over and over again until you actually come to believe it. There was nothing "different" about you that made your parents decide to dislike you or treat you unfairly while they loved your little sister to pieces (and right in front of your eyes). Many firstborns I've counseled honestly felt there was something about them that caused their parents to pick on them and resent them. This simply isn't so, and if you can't believe that, stand in front of the mirror for as long as it takes and tell yourself over and over, "It's not my fault."

It really isn't.

But you also need to realize that what happened as you were growing up is seen in your mind's eye through the lens of your own perception. Different children in the same family will perceive the same event completely differently. Each person's perception depends on their own private logic. Yet whether that perception of the event is authentic or not, says psychologist Alfred Adler, it is real to the child.

Also, keep in mind that a firstborn is more influenced by who is above them in the family chain. Therefore, what a parent says and does is far more influential for a firstborn than for any other birth order. Firstborns are the guinea pig—the children parents "practice on." They are the ones who get in trouble for not watching the younger siblings more carefully. They are the ones who are often asked to stay home and

137

babysit and have to give up what they want to do to please a parent. And all of these happenings can easily lead to a firstborn's resentment toward parents.

Make a Conscious Decision to Forgive

If you wait around hoping that one of these days you're going to wake up feeling better about things, chances are you never will. And even if you do, look at all the time you're wasting while you're waiting. That alone would drive any firstborn crazy.

If you're holding on to bitterness and unforgiveness, the person you're really hurting is yourself. There will be no joy in your life, you'll be a miserable person to be around, and others will notice and step away—including your friends, your co-workers, your spouse, and your own children. Holding on to your bitterness causes more than emotional and relational hurt; it can cause all sorts of physical problems too. Ulcers, high blood pressure, chronic headaches, and even diseases such as cancer have been linked to refusing to let go of bitterness and pain. When you learn to forgive others, you're really helping yourself.

Forgiveness, for the most part, is something you do and not something you feel. It is an act of the will, not the emotions.

Keep Busy

Okay, a little caution here—after all, you are a firstborn. I'm not saying, "Take on more projects than you can possibly handle." Don't overwhelm yourself with work that will keep you busy twenty-five hours a day. But do get involved in enough outside projects so you don't sit around and think about how miserable you are. Instead, focus your thoughts on constructive projects so the weeds of bitterness and anger don't have any more room to grow. If you help others (volunteer for Meals on Wheels, give of your time to a nursing home, etc.), you have less time to focus on your life and your problems. When you see the struggles that others have, sometimes your own problems pale in comparison. As you help others, you'll find yourself smiling more, interacting more—and liking yourself a lot more.

Get Out There and Give It a Shot

So many firstborns, as discouraged perfectionists, aren't living up to their potential. They aren't taking risks because the messages of a critical-eyed parent are playing in their head: *You can't do that.*

But why can't you? You're an adult now, so who's stopping you? Why not get out there and take a risk? Show yourself—and others—that you're a capable, intelligent person. Go after your dreams.

Lisa, a thirtyish firstborn wife and mother, was practically crippled by her lack of self-confidence and self-respect as a result of a critical-eyed father.

She had married right out of college, and even though she didn't have any children for several years, she never worked—primarily because of her lack of self-esteem.

She was aghast when I suggested she find a job, at least part-time. Why, she could never see herself even looking for a job, much less finding one. But because she really did want to change and step away from her critical-eyed past, she finally agreed she'd give it her best shot.

139

To her surprise, she found a job working two days a week as a receptionist in a dentist's office. The first day she almost decided to call in and say that she'd changed her mind about taking the position or, at the very least, that she'd come down with the flu. But to her credit, she didn't.

Her husband was proud of her but didn't think she'd last more than a couple weeks. To be honest, neither did I. But a month went by, and then another one, and she stuck with it. A couple times she caught and corrected scheduling mistakes. Her self-confidence grew when her boss told her he appreciated the job she was doing.

She could hardly believe it when her boss called her into the office and asked if she'd consider working full-time. She thanked him but told him that wasn't what she really wanted to do. He said he understood and agreed to give her a raise in pay anyway. That fifty cents an hour might sound like a small thing, but it was big evidence to her that she was doing a good job.

That success on the job helped her turn her life around. She became more confident in other areas of her life too, and she found that she was less critical of her own children.

But guess what? None of that would have happened if she hadn't been willing to try. Are you willing?

Get Professional Counseling

If you've tried everything I've suggested and more, and you still can't get rid of those feelings of resentment and bitterness, find a competent therapist and seek help in that way. There's nothing wrong with asking for professional help, and it certainly doesn't mean you have failed or fallen short of the mark. But I know it's hard for firstborns to seek professional help—after all, by nature you're in charge of the world. Seeking help is seen as a sign of weakness and failure, and firstborns—heaven forbid—should never fail. But if you're a wise firstborn, you'll learn to recognize your weaknesses, improve on them, and play off your strengths.

Sidestepping the Naysayers—for Good

I'll say it bluntly. You are under no obligation to believe or even listen to those who condemn you. Firstborns are often so busy living up to everyone else's standards that you don't stop to figure out what you really want out of life. You've been living up to the expectations of parents, teachers, friends, etc., for so long that it's hard to even comprehend anything else. And that means you tend to believe what anyone else says about you:

> "He said I'm a terrible writer. It must be true, so I suppose I'll have to give it up."
>
> "She said I'm the world's worst actress. Too bad, because I've always loved the theater, but, well, no sense hanging around and making a fool of myself."
>
> "He said I'll never be able to play soccer again—at least not well—since I got hurt. Might as well just give away my ball."
>
> "She said I'll never learn to play the piano, and I'm sure she's right. I'm just not cut out for a career in music."

I'll never forget a conversation I had with Hall of Fame college basketball coach Lute Olson. I asked him, "Hey, Coach, what about criticism? How do you handle it?"

"Depends on who's doing the criticizing," he said.

All of us need to keep that simple concept in mind. No one likes criticism, but when you get hammered from someone you respect, it bothers you more—and it should.

Who are the critical-eyed people in your life? How invested are they in your life? What do they have to gain—or lose—by hammering you?

Who says you have to listen to the naysayers anyway? You're not living your life to please them—or are you? If you are, it's time to ask yourself, *What do I really want out of life?* After all, do the naysayers really have your best interests in mind, or could their motives be less than honorable?

Also, are you making unreasonable demands of yourself? Jacking up the high bar of life? Doing so is in a firstborn's nature. Self-image is a particular problem for firstborns because you are always being asked to do and be the best. The firstborn who knows she is not as attractive as her younger sister will exaggerate her own flaws and imperfections. The oldest boy who knows his younger brother is better at football will come to see himself as the no-talent klutz.

Most people aren't either perfect tens or nerds. They are simply average, somewhere in between.

Because of growing up firstborn and being in the limelight, you often believe you are worth something only when you are noticed, when you can be in control of any situation, or when you can look down on others. The truth is that you don't have to do or be anything other than who you are. You have worth because of who you are—a human created by the almighty God in his image. Telling yourself that you have to measure up to anything other than who you are is a lie. When you tell yourself this lie, you're picking apart your own self-worth and holding yourself back.

So if I asked you what you want to do with your life, what would you say? You probably can tell me in no uncertain terms exactly what you want to do. "I'm going to get my PhD by the time I'm 25. Then I'm going to teach at a university. On the side, I'm going to write books and have my first published novel by the time I'm 30. . . ."

But what if I asked you, "Why did you make those choices?"

Now we're probably on shaky ground. You're not quite so sure of yourself. Maybe you're an attorney because that's what your father wanted you to be. Or maybe you're in dental school because that's what makes your mom smile. Or maybe you're a teacher

> Are you making unreasonable demands on yourself? Jacking up the high bar of life?

because that's a family occupation and well respected.

Your mom and dad may be long gone or in a different state. You're no longer under their control or in their house, but are you still living for them? Or are you living for yourself?

Today is the day to decide what *you* want to do and to stick to your guns (especially if you're a pleaser). Take a realistic look at yourself. Evaluate your strengths and talents and ask yourself these kinds of questions:

1. What do I *really* enjoy doing?
2. When do other people compliment me?
3. In what subjects did I do well in school?
4. What comes easy for me?
5. What is hard for me?
6. If I could change my life in any way, what would I do differently?

If you're a pleaser, the most difficult thing for you to do will be to act on what you discover about yourself. Don't let any critical-eyed parents or friends be naysayers in your plan. It's a very different thing to *listen* to what someone has to say and to *believe* it's the only opinion that counts.

Firstborns, more than middleborn or younger children, are the ones most susceptible to what many folks call a "midlife crisis." That's because firstborns spend their lives trying to please everyone else and to be who other people want them to be. Then they reach age 40 or 45 and suddenly think, *Hey, I've never done anything for myself.* That's why so many midlife firstborns suddenly change jobs, move across the country, begin to drive yellow Corvettes (and get caught speeding), and even change spouses for a younger model. What they're saying is, *I'm tired of everyone expecting me to do this and that. I want to be free, without anyone telling me what to do.*

Don't get caught in the trap of rebelling against others' critical eyes. Learn to be as honest with yourself as you can in all things, great and small, on a day-to-day basis. Don't try to be who you aren't.

Flaw Pickers Anonymous

If you've ever been to an AA meeting, or any other Something Anonymous meeting, you know that the members always start out with, "Hi, my name is So-and-So, and I'm an [alcoholic/drug addict/etc.]."

Well, what about Flaw Pickers Anonymous? Just come right out and admit it. As a firstborn, you tend to pick out the flaw in any situation or any person. But guess who you're the hardest on? Yourself.

"Hi, my name is Shauna, and I'm a firstborn and a flaw picker."

"Hi, my name is Dave, and I'm a firstborn and a flaw picker."

Are you afraid to step out of the house without your makeup done to perfection? Do you sweat thinking about presentations, and then overprepare? Are you your own worst critic and harshest judge?

Now tell me. Are you really as bad as all that? Or is your flaw-picking nature working overtime to discourage you?

In his book *How to Raise Your Self-Esteem*, Dr. Nathaniel Branden suggests that you can learn to be honest with yourself by using a technique of "sentence completion."[4] For example, he suggests completing the sentence "I like myself least when I..." Add everything you can think of. Be as honest as you can possibly be, and don't worry about hurting your feelings.

After you've done that, turn the question around and write, "I like myself most when I..." Again, list everything you can think of. Then resolve that you are going to act in ways that make you like yourself.

If you've become the critical eye in your own life, isn't it about time to cut yourself some slack? You do not have to be what anyone else expects or wants you to be. Just be who and what you really are.

7

The Firstborn Advantage at Home

How to use your firstborn skills to strengthen your relationships with your spouse and children (who may be the same or a different birth order than you).

There are two types of firstborns: those who like to be in charge, and those who do everything they can to please you.

Which one are you?

The *powerful firstborn* needs to be in control and is on the defensive to make sure no one usurps his role. You hear statements from him like, "I'm the head of the home here" and "You will do what I say." These controllers stay away from personal connection because, underneath all their outward signs of power, they fear losing control. They're critical, they're perfectionistic, and they expect everyone around them to toe the line *exactly the way they want it toed.*

What are they really saying? "I only count in life when I'm in charge, when I'm running the show, when the focus is on me." The powerful firstborn has never grown up from the little boy (or girl) who had his parents' complete attention—before the other siblings were born, that is.

The powerful firstborn usually does very well in business. But the same skills that make him so successful in his job can kill his relationships at home. Maybe his employees don't mind being ordered around, but do you think his wife wants to be? I've never once had a wife come into my counseling office and say, "Oh, Doc, I just *love* the way my husband controls me."

These firstborns don't have to be aggressive to be powerful; they can also be shy and moody. That's a form of control too. But they are all masters at manipulating others to do exactly what they want to do, when they want to do it. A controlling wife runs her husband's schedule, not giving him a moment to breathe when he's home. A controlling husband and father walks in the door, and immediately everyone starts to lower their voices for fear of offending him or causing a tirade. And then he exerts his powerful personality even more when he refuses to let his wife know what's on his mind and keeps her guessing.

The *pleaser firstborn* spends her days trying to juggle all the balls that will keep everyone happy. That's her main goal in life: to keep everyone happy and to keep the peace. Because this firstborn was often beaten down by a critical parent, she is saying, in effect, "Okay, I'll do what you want. I don't want to cause a ripple in the waters here."

The pleaser often doesn't think very highly of herself. She's insecure, unsure of her place in the world. Her only value is in what she does for others. And it isn't long before everyone in the family will take advantage of that. Approval means everything to her; she's crushed without it. As a result, she makes decisions that sometimes aren't wise (such as letting her firstborn daughter spend four hundred dollars at J. Crew when the family can't afford it). And then what happens when her powerful husband finds out? There's a volcanic explosion.

Why do I mention these two personality types in a chapter about relationships at home? Because opposites attract. Most often, powerful people marry pleasers. It's no wonder, then, that they are often at cross purposes in marriage.[1]

I want to stop right here, though, to note a very important gender-related pattern with firstborns. You may already have noticed it, based on the examples I've used in this chapter. Every firstborn—male or female—will always notice what *should* be but isn't done, and how perfectly (or not) something is done. But there is a vast difference between the genders and the way they respond to this perfectionistic tendency.

Firstborn males will tend to be controllers. The firstborn male will be the first one to notice, for example, that the garbage needs to be taken out. However, his tendency will be to order someone else to do it. He'll also be the one who notices when his partner should lose some weight, change a hairstyle, or stop talking so much. The firstborn male can easily be a sexist chauvinist who uses his firstborn personality and demands to get his own way, especially with the opposite sex.

Firstborn females will tend to be pleasers. They see everything that needs to be done and know that they can do those jobs and do them well, so they work hard to smooth everyone else's path in life, often at great sacrifice to themselves. So if a husband doesn't get a job done that he says he will, the firstborn wife sighs and thinks, *Well, I guess I'll just have to do it myself.* But whose job is it, really? Why are you doing it for him?

It's the firstborn female, in particular, who tends to carry a marriage. She's so dependable that she teaches her husband to be irresponsible. And who pays the price? She does. And then the marriage does.

Because of these gender-related tendencies of firstborns, a marriage between two firstborns can turn into a free-for-all in which the husband is controlling and the wife is running a marathon to please him. In the long run, the controlling husband may think he's winning, but there will come a time when the exhausted wife will think, *There's got to be more to life than this—and him.* And from there, it's often a steady downward slide into "Have your attorney call my attorney."

Does it have to be that way? Certainly not. A marriage for a lifetime is all about finding a healthy balance of give-and-take in your relationship. The firstborn male needs to learn to put his wife first; the firstborn female needs to learn to think of herself and her exhaustion level.

Your View of Life Has Everything to Do with It

If you're a firstborn, you know you're perfectionistic, exacting, organized, orderly, analytical, and goal oriented. The way you relate to your spouse and your children has everything to do with the way you see life. And the way you see life (the private logic that you formed at an early age, which tells you how to think and respond to what happens to you) has everything to do with the way your parents related to you.

Did your parents strive for perfection or pursue excellence? Was it okay to fail? Did life go on, or did it stop if you failed at something or made a mistake? Could you and your parents laugh at your goof ups?

As a result, do you tend toward the pleaser or powerful firstborn in temperament? It is only as you understand your strengths and weaknesses that you can strengthen your relationship skills at home.

Also, was your father actively involved in your life as a child? If he wasn't, you may be more of a person who keeps others at an arm's length. You may not be comfortable with relationships or with letting anyone close enough to see the real you. After all, if you're succeeding in business and making the big bucks, you're providing for the family, right? And you're accumulating enough big-people toys, clothes, and cars to show others that you're doing well, aren't you?

But is your wife or husband left in the dust and living the lifestyle of a married single? Do the two of you share the same house, bedroom, and children, but each do your own thing?

If your parents weren't both actively involved in raising you, you'll have trouble working together with your spouse to raise your child. This is particularly true of the firstborn male, who struggles with relating to others anyway.

When you walked down that aisle, you didn't just marry your spouse. Both sets of parents—and all the baggage that came with them—were in on the deal too.

It's fascinating that firstborn women who have strong, successful careers can be jellyfish pleasers in marriage. How can

> Firstborn women who have strong, successful careers can be jellyfish pleasers in marriage.

that happen? Do you think that's what she saw patterned in her own home? And if the firstborn male saw his dad treat his wife carelessly, how do you think that firstborn is going to treat his wife?

What goes around certainly does come around. And it affects everyone in the home.

If You're a Pleaser Firstborn . . .

If you're a pleaser firstborn (women typically fall into this role because of their relational nature), you're going to exhaust yourself physically and emotionally trying to fulfill everyone's wants and needs. Trying to meet all those expectations is a recipe for disaster. Even worse, because you've been so busily pleasing everyone, that's what they expect. But it's not your job to take on everyone's work, only your own.

What can you do to get out of the trap of being a pleaser?

Learn to express yourself. You don't need to be the silent, suffering martyr. Speak up. Tell your family how you feel—that you're tired of doing everything for them. It makes you feel used and like a personal slave instead of a family member.

Make a list of things you do for your spouse and your children, and cut back. Are they things that family members could do for themselves? If so, why are *you* doing them?

Get others to pitch in and do their fair share of the work. If they don't pitch in, leave the tasks undone (as difficult

Who Does What around Your House?

Duty	You	Spouse	Kids	Shared
Mowing and watering the lawn	☐	☐	☐	☐
Doing the laundry	☐	☐	☐	☐
Fixing dinner	☐	☐	☐	☐
Shoveling snow (residents of Tucson may ignore this one)	☐	☐	☐	☐
Helping kids with homework	☐	☐	☐	☐
Keeping bathroom clean	☐	☐	☐	☐
Tucking kids into bed	☐	☐	☐	☐
Keeping cars in good shape	☐	☐	☐	☐
Taking kids to doctors' appointments	☐	☐	☐	☐
Straightening, dusting, etc.	☐	☐	☐	☐
Making the beds	☐	☐	☐	☐
Feeding pets	☐	☐	☐	☐
Doing dog plop patrol	☐	☐	☐	☐

Give yourself 10 points for each thing you do. I'll wait while you add them up.

90–130: Either you're a single parent or you're not getting much help. Are you a pleaser? You need to make some changes and ask others to help out more.

70–80: You still do too much. Whose fault is that, I ask you?

40–60: That sounds just about right.

0–30: Are you sure you're a firstborn?

as that is for a pleaser firstborn). When your husband doesn't have clean boxers to wear to work, he just might have an inkling to do the laundry that night. When your kids show up at school with no lunch because they forgot to pack it, oh well. Going hungry for one lunch won't kill them—but it will teach them a lesson not soon forgotten.

Remember that you are responsible only for what you do, not for what anyone else does—or doesn't do. Let the chips fall where they may. Experience is a very good teacher.

Remember that you can't do it all. You're only one person, with the same twenty-four hours a day that everyone else has. You need to lower your own expectations of yourself and learn to say no.

I know one woman who spent more time in her yellow minivan than she did at home, running all the kids in the neighborhood from one activity to the next. The minivan wasn't really a taxi, but everyone seemed to act like it was. Think that woman was a pleaser? Does she remind you of you? If so, now's the time to get tough and take action. It's for your own good as well as everyone else's. Your spouse and children need to buck up and accept some responsibility.

If You're a Powerful Firstborn . . .

If you're a powerful firstborn, you have very high expectations of yourself. And you tend to have those high expectations for everyone around you.

"Why isn't the house clean? What did you do all day?"

"You can't tie your shoes yet? You're 4. Michael could tie his shoes by the time he was 4. You're not trying hard enough."

"I needed that for today's presentation."

You also have a need to control others. And yours is the only right way. You don't see a great need for communication because you're always telling everyone what you want from them.

Yes, you're a master of detail; that's what got you all your job promotions. But are you expecting everyone else, including your 2-year-old, to be as precise as you? What are you gaining in the long run—other than family division and a spouse and children who run the other way when they see you coming?

How can you use your skills to your best advantage as a powerful firstborn?

Listen first, before you open your mouth. What you hear may surprise you, and you may even change your mind about what you were going to say. Remember the old adage: "If you can't say something nice, don't say anything at all."

Adopt the other person's point of view. Get behind your family members' eyes. How do they see you and your demands? Are you frustrating your children? Exasperating your wife?

Delegate authority. Saying "I guess I have to do it myself if I want it done right" doesn't make the rest of your family members feel very good about themselves. But doing a job together or delegating responsibility says, "I believe you can do it. In fact, I *know* you can do it. Let's do it together. You do that, and I'll do this, and we'll get it done quickly." Will the job be done as precisely as you might have done it yourself? Most likely not. But you'll be building your family's confidence level in themselves and in you as a leader.

Bury the bone deep, and don't dig it up again. Don't resurrect all the things family members have done wrong and beat them over the head with them. Would you want someone to do that to you? People feel bad enough about their mistakes (and they remember them much more than you think). Instead, treat the past as the past and move on.

Rein in your criticism. It hurts your family far more than you could ever know. The fallout will greatly influence their relationships and their feelings of self-worth all throughout their lives.

Keep an eagle eye on your expectations. Just because you have high expectations for yourself doesn't mean everyone else has to live up to them. You are precise and exacting, but does that mean everyone in your family has to be? Others may not be as "perfect" as you, but they all have something to contribute. Don't miss out on that.

Let's say you're having trouble getting family members to help you at home. You ask your son to mow the lawn. But he knows that if he does, you're going to come out and redo it because he didn't do it exactly the way you wanted him to. So do you think your son will want to mow the lawn, or will he find something better to do? If your daughter makes her bed, but then you come in right behind her, tear it all apart, and remake it so it's "perfect," she'll decide to just let you do it from now on. If they don't try, they can't fail, right?

And you know, they're right. Why *should* they waste their time and effort doing something that you're only going to end up doing over? You're actually trapping yourself into extra work. Worrying too much about the minor details of life will drive everyone else crazy, and it will put you in the role of doing every job because no one else will measure up.

Who cares, frankly, if the sandwiches for lunch aren't cut exactly at perpendicular angles? And why does your husband have to pick up his dry cleaning today when it would be right on his way to work tomorrow—and then he could get home earlier tonight? Is the world going to end if your wife leaves her makeup scattered across the counter and happens to use your toothpaste because she's out?

Look at it this way: your standards are just that—*your* standards. But does that make everyone else's wrong? No.

If you want your son to mow the lawn once a week, but he thinks every two weeks is plenty, why not accept his standard? (I doubt your neighbors will be out there measuring the length of your grass. And if *you* are, you've got more problems than I thought. You'd better get to a psychiatrist quick.)

If your daughter's room is always messy and you find yourself constantly cleaning up after her, make a deal: if she'll clean her room twice a week, the rest of the time you won't nag her about it. In other words, learn to accept her standards. (Up to a certain point, of course. If you call the Orkin man but he won't go into her room because his insurance carrier won't allow it, then it's time for action.)

Firstborn, you can't do it all. You need to learn to delegate and to trust others to get the job done—even if it's not to your perfect standard. But then, what about life is really perfect anyway?

How Birth Order Affects Marriage

Think about your family for a minute. Whom do you butt heads with the most? Is it your spouse? A child? What birth order is that person? It's highly likely that he or she is a firstborn. That's because the person you're most likely to butt heads with is the person with the same birth order.

> The person you're most likely to butt heads with is the person with the same birth order.

So if you've married a firstborn, look out.

When Firstborn Marries Firstborn

You know the personality of firstborns because you are one. And if you married a firstborn, it's inevitable that there will be a strong clashing of wills. You're both stubborn ("determined" is a nicer way of putting it), detail oriented (which means you'll fight over things that wouldn't even make a ripple for other birth orders, like where to put the sprinkler in the yard), and perfectionistic. You're serious about life and goal oriented. You are analytical and know exactly what the right thing to do is. But what if your firstborn spouse also knows what the right thing to do is—and it's something very different from your plan?

No wonder it's tough for two strong, dominant personalities to be married. Is it impossible? No. You just need to learn how to negotiate a truce and to bring peace into your relationship. Otherwise you'll be in a continual power struggle.

How can two firstborns live more in harmony?

Divvy up tasks and assign roles to figure out who should be in charge of what, given your particular strengths. Then stick to your specific areas of control. That way each of you can be king or queen over your respective areas. The key is not to step into your spouse's areas for any reason or to assume control of their tasks.

Stop criticizing. "If only you did . . ." "You should have done . . ." Whatever happened is over and done with. Criticism does nothing other than discourage your partner and make them angry and bitter. The entire climate in a home can change if both spouses decide to shut their mouths.

Don't redo things that your spouse has already done. Sure, you might be able to make an improvement, but does it really matter? Is it that important if the shrimp is arranged a certain way on a dish?

Let your "do it my way" hit the highway. When you got married, you agreed to "become one." And that means giving up some privileges, including this big one. Instead of thinking about what you want, work on pleasing your spouse.

Lighten up. Life doesn't always have to be so serious. What you're fixing for dinner and who's fixing dinner won't make a difference a few days down the road, once the food has digested in your stomach, so why make it a big deal?

In other words, stop the competition. There's no room in marriage for "I'm doing it my way." Although you are predisposed to be a great reformer of your spouse, don't go there. What attracted you to them in the first place? Most likely they still have those same qualities, so why are you trying to change your spouse? Trying to change a firstborn male doesn't work; it only irritates him. Trying to tell a driven firstborn female what to do doesn't work; it only angers her. Trying to change your spouse will be like two mountain goats butting heads for the territorial rights to your marriage.

> Marriage is not a contest that you win. It's a relationship.

Marriage is not a contest that you win. It's a relationship. There's no place for a win-lose philosophy.

When Firstborn Marries Middleborn

Middleborns are very accommodating and flexible. Because they never had Mom and Dad to themselves, compromise became their way of life, and they were squeezed in the middle at home between youngest and oldest, so they're used to not being noticed. They're used to their opinions not really being asked. And because they're in the middle, no one has paid much attention to them. So when the firstborn is strong, is opinionated (okay, sometimes plain bossy), and holds firm to the "I'm always right" philosophy, what usually happens? The middleborn spouse acquiesces.

On the surface, that sounds great to you as the firstborn. *Hey, I got my way*, you think, and go on, smiling, to conquer the next mountain.

160

But someone pays for that, and it's the middle child. Since the middle child is most likely to have a problem telling you how they really feel, they often experience a building of resentment and bitterness. It builds and builds until finally the middle child realizes, *I've been spending my whole life trying to make the oceans of life smooth for him/her. What about me? Don't I matter?*

What can firstborns do to make the most of marriage with a middle child?

Regularly ask their opinion. Middleborns have much wisdom to share, but they are rarely asked. And because they've been stuck in the middle at home, they're not likely to offer their opinion without you asking. It might take several times of you asking, in fact, for them to risk sharing an opinion. Then they might say something like, "Oh, that's fine." But don't stop there. Tell your spouse you really want to know what they think because it's important to you.

Make them feel special—because they are. You wouldn't be where you are (and you certainly wouldn't have as many friends) without your middleborn spouse.

Include them on decisions. Process your thoughts with them. Just because they don't leap to conclusions as quickly as you do doesn't mean they aren't intelligent or don't have wisdom to offer. Trust me—you'll never go wrong with this approach with a middle child.

One of the most wonderful things about having a marriage with a middleborn is that they thrive on relationships. Friends are their greatest ally. The firstborn who thinks he knows all and sees all would be smart to check with his middleborn spouse, who has a nose for people like a bird dog has a nose for a pheasant in an Iowa cornfield. The middleborn's gut feelings and relational skills will keep many a firstborn out of the woods. No wonder middleborns have the best track record for building a loving marriage.

If two babies are married to each other, they'll glide through life, never getting anything done—until they get in trouble. Then it's always the other spouse's fault. Rarely does a baby's finger point back at himself. But you know the old adage: "If you point a finger at someone else, three of your fingers are pointing back at you."

If two firstborns are married to each other, they'll knock heads and may end up competing with each other unless they choose areas where they each can be the "expert."

But put a middleborn with either of these personalities, and the ocean is much clearer for sailing. That's because middle children have spent their entire lives seeing both sides of the issue. They've negotiated the waters between older and younger siblings and have often had to drift between the two as the peacemaker. They are loyal friends and great compromisers—the balancers of life.

Funny how birth order works, isn't it?

When Firstborn Marries Lastborn

I know a lot about this one because I'm a youngest child, and my wife, Sande, is a firstborn. We're a living example of how this type of birth-order marriage can work—and work well. The youngest child is a great asset to the firstborn in a very natural way. They're about as opposite as you can get.

Firstborns tend to sweat the details; babies have the ability to roll with the punches. The baby takes things in stride and doesn't get worked up over much in life. The baby also has a great sense of humor. (Comedians Jim Carrey, Drew Carey, Martin Short, Chevy Chase, Jay Leno, Whoopi Goldberg, Stephen Colbert, and Ellen DeGeneres are all babies of the family.) So the firstborn anchors the baby (when he could go floating up like a balloon toward the heavens and forget what is down here on earth), and the baby lightens up the firstborn, taking the edge off life.

If there could be any match made in heaven, this would be it. But does that mean there isn't trouble every once in a while in paradise?

Consider this scenario. Let's say your wife is a baby of the family. She has just seen a copper sink on *Martha Stewart Living*, so she's making plans. After all, she's remodeling the kitchen, and that copper sink would be just the ticket to spruce it up. But you, as a firstborn husband, know that the sink alone costs $3,700 and wouldn't be in your budget—in fact, not even close. You've been to Home Depot zillions of times, and you've never seen a sink that cost so much. You're convinced it's made out of gold nuggets instead of copper.

> Firstborns tend to sweat the details; babies have the ability to roll with the punches.

But the baby of the family is illogical. She's used to instant gratification. After all, because she was the youngest, big brother always paid attention to her and got her toys while Mom scrambled to feed her first.

So your wife begins the "I want it, and I want it now" plea.

What's your response, as a firstborn? "If you want it that badly, I don't mind. But we don't have that kind of money in our budget. We're going to have to start saving for it on a regular basis. Let's pay for it in cash and save the interest."

Babies are the ones who want the most expensive car—the red convertible with the gold trim. Firstborns are the ones who'd rather have the more conservative-looking car that will have longer shelf value.

What can firstborns do to make the most of marriage with a baby?

Filter through the "I want" requests to determine what is a need, what is a want, and what can wait. But take care not to shatter your spouse's dreams in the process.

Don't pick up the slack for chores that your spouse has agreed to do. In other words, if your lastborn husband was supposed to bring donuts for his Saturday morning outing with his buddies but forgot to pick them up, don't rescue him by reminding him on Friday of his responsibility or running out at 9 a.m. to Dunkin' Donuts. It's *his* outing, right? Let his buddies remind him of his responsibility when they're hungry. The message will get across, and you won't be the nag.

Gently bring your freewheeling spouse back to earth when needed. For instance, let's say your baby-of-the-family wife insists that she's always making the minimum payment on her Visa card, so everything's okay. There comes a time when the practical firstborn husband needs to say, "Honey, I think we've agreed that in this marriage I let you do things that you're better at than I am. But you have to admit that I'm better at finances than you. . . ." And then proceed to show your spouse that if she pays just the minimum payment for four lifetimes, the bill will never be paid off, and you'll be in financial trouble. So in the best interest of your family, that practice has to stop now. Otherwise you'll be paying 33 percent interest, which almost rivals loan sharking. In the same way, if the baby-of-the-family husband shows up twenty minutes late to his wife's VP awards banquet, he won't exactly impress the board members and the president of her company. The smart firstborn wife, knowing her husband's proclivity for being late, will tell him that he needs to be at the banquet at 7:00 instead of 7:30. Now that's using birth order to your advantage and playing smart.

Be careful with your criticism. Criticism can crush babies' spirits. They may look happy-go-lucky, but they are tenderhearted and live to please you.

Work on making decisions together. Firstborns are used to going solo. But you need the balance that your baby-of-the-family spouse brings to the table.

Sit back and enjoy the ride. What an adventure it will be!

The baby is spontaneous and carefree; the firstborn is the planner and organizer. But somewhere in the mix lies a happy medium. If either the firstborn is too dominant or the baby is too carefree and freewheeling, they'll have major problems (like a lot of credit card debt). But if they work together, they'll tend to balance each other out.

Are You Just Talking—or Communicating?

One of the most important things you can do for your marriage is learn to be a good communicator. This is particularly important for firstborn males to understand.

You're an extremely competent guy, Mr. Firstborn. You might be an engineer or an attorney. You might use your words all the time to win cases, make sales, clinch successful presentations, etc. But then you get home, and what happens? You shut down. You're done with your word count for the day.

But what about your wife? Is she done? It's doubtful, since women use three and a half times as many words a day as men. When a guy finishes talking to his co-workers, his word count is done for the day. But his wife? She's just getting started. (Especially if she's a baby of the family and she's used to attention. For babies, social interaction is the name of the game.) Can you see why communication is such a big deal in marriage? And why a difference in communication styles causes more trouble in marriage than anything else?

If you're a firstborn male, you need to understand that your wife (whether firstborn, middle child, or baby of the family) needs your words. A few grunts over dinner and a "fine" when asked about your day aren't enough to satisfy your wife.

If she's a firstborn, she might be happy with a quick outline of your day, with some highlighted points—in other words, a few words will do. She may even be busy with an internal dialogue of her own. *Okay, if I get the laundry done right after dinner, then I can start that project for the school committee, get Karyn a bath, and read over my notes while I watch her.*

If she's a middle child, she probably won't push you, but she's wondering, *Why won't he talk to me? Don't I matter? I guess I'm not interesting enough to share anything with. Or maybe he thinks I won't understand it. (Sigh.) Oh well. Life goes on.*

If she's a baby, she needs words, sentences, and paragraphs from you. She needs you to speak in complete, flowing thoughts and give stories, although it's in your very nature to speak in sound bites. She needs the whole enchilada.

But no matter her birth order, *every* woman needs words in order to feel close to her husband. Every woman thrives on communication.

And let's be blunt: by nature we men in general (not just firstborn men) aren't very good at it.

But does that get us off the hook? No. When you said, "I do," you made a promise to love and cherish this woman for a lifetime. And an important part of that promise is getting behind her eyes to see how she views life.

Why Not Combine Forces?

Each of you has specific strengths and specific weaknesses. So instead of competing, why not bond together to use each other's strengths and shore up each other's weaknesses? Marriage, after all, is a team effort—not a show of two people acting on their own. But in order for your trust level to be high enough to act as one, you not only have to talk, you have to *communicate*. You have to understand what the other is not only saying but also feeling.

You also have to know each other well enough to know your strengths and weaknesses. (In my book *Be Your Own*

Shrink,[2] I talk at length about how to identify your strengths and weaknesses.)

In marriage, it's important to divide up tasks according to your strengths, not according to what you're "supposed to do." Who is the bill payer? For many families, it's the male by tradition. But who says it has to be the male? Frankly, a lot of females are much more detail oriented. If one person is computer illiterate and the other is a whiz, figure out whether it's easier to pay checks by hand or online. In other words, work together to divvy up the tasks so neither of you feels overwhelmed. Marriage is supposed to be an equal partnership—not one person dumping all the work on the other.

> It's important to divide up tasks according to your strengths, not according to what you're "supposed to do."

All you're doing is assessing your strengths and weaknesses, then making decisions of who does what based on that evaluation. If you are both working in your areas of strength, you'll be much happier, less critical of each other, and more understanding of each other's idiosyncrasies because you appreciate your respective talents.

You don't always have to agree on everything. Men and women are different. Sande gets her nails done at a salon; I do mine at a red light. Sande goes to the ladies' room in groups of 10 or 123; I prefer to go alone to the men's room. That doesn't make one of us better than the other—just different.

No matter the birth orders you and your spouse have, if you keep in mind the following principles, you'll have a smoother-sailing relationship.

Marriage is not about being "better"; it's about a partnership. It's not a competition; it's two people working together, in love, for their common good. You won't be perfect, and your spouse won't be perfect. You won't always agree, and that's okay. But you can work together, using your strengths and shoring up your weaknesses for the good of your family.

Marriage is about understanding your spouse's feelings and their perspective. It's caring enough to take the time to listen and to truly communicate.

Marriage is about making the other person feel special. How often do you go out of your way to do something special for your spouse? Firstborns can be so focused on the task that they can forget about the person. So why not sit down and write a short note right now. Or send an email. Stop at a coffee shop. Get a few sweetheart roses for your sweetheart. Buy tickets to a movie.

I know your life is busy—firstborns have a lot to do, managing the world as they do. But how about taking some time for the most important relationship of all—with your spouse of a lifetime?

Different Strokes for Different Little Folks

You don't even have to look at your kids. You *know* your firstborn, middleborn, and baby are completely different from each other. (For more on just how different they are, you'll find *The Birth Order Book* extremely helpful.) It's no wonder that the interactions between you as a firstborn parent and each child will be quite different. The smart parent

169

will learn to take advantage of her firstborn skills by becoming aware of unique relational patterns between each birth order.

Firstborn Parent with Firstborn Child

If the national average for the age a child walks is 12 months, you expect your firstborn to walk at 11 months, 20 days. If the national average for the age a child begins to read is 4, you want your child to begin to read at 3. Because you are a new parent when you have your firstborn, you overdo it a little. In fact, you overdo just about every aspect of parenting. If you don't believe that's true, and if you have three children, stop and think for a minute about how you treated your firstborn versus how you treated your third-born. By the time your thirdborn came around, you realized it wouldn't kill him if he ate some dirt. Neither would it kill him if he ate plant mulch or dead ladybugs. When your firstborn did that, you ran toward her screaming, yanked the dead ladybugs out of her mouth, and rinsed her mouth seven times.

So it shouldn't surprise you that your firstborn became cautious—and a perfectionist. And because you spent so much time with her, it shouldn't surprise you that she became more comfortable with adults than with her peers.

Guess the Birth Order

When the phone rings in your home, who is it usually for?

firstborn
middleborn
lastborn

Your son is very concerned about a crease in his blue shirt. Who is he?

firstborn
middleborn
lastborn

"I just can't do it right now. I have to prepare first."

firstborn
middleborn
lastborn[3]

170

After all, she spent the most time with you, the parent, as her role model.

You may have pushed her harder than you should have. You know that now. You may have redone things for her that you should have left alone. You hovered a little too much. Criticized a little too much.

You tended to project your own unfulfilled dreams and wishes on her. For example, you signed her up for violin lessons because you always wanted to play the violin. And you insisted she stay with it for two years, even though she hated it. Then you discovered how individualistic each of your children was after baby #2 was born.

> If the national average for the age a child walks is 12 months, you expect your firstborn to walk at 11 months, 20 days.

Whom did you butt heads with most? Hands down, it was your firstborn—because she's the most like you. Yes, you understand her the best, but she can also drive you crazy. Yet she, because of her perfectionistic nature, needs your encouragement even more than your other children. But she needs real encouragement, not false praise. Encouragement focuses on the act or job done well; praise focuses on the actor (for example, "You're the best guy in the world because you did a good job on that"). If you're a critical-eyed parent (or your spouse is), you need to be especially aware of how deeply your criticism will become ingrained in your firstborn's personality.

What does your firstborn need from you?

5 Tips for Parenting a Firstborn

1. *Realize that firstborns have a particular need to know exactly what the rules are in any situation.* Take time to lay out the rules from A to Z. Her personality demands it.

2. *Don't reinforce your firstborn's already ingrained perfectionistic tendencies.* Don't improve on everything he says and does. Don't "should" him. He does this enough to himself anyway. Accept what he has done instead of trying to improve on it.

   Also, watch your own critical eye. Firstborns are extremely sensitive to criticism and being corrected. Let your firstborn try a skill on his own first, and wait until he asks for help. Then give a few tips, but don't hover. Gently encourage. For example, if your firstborn is working on a math problem, don't jump in with an explanation. See what he can figure out first. If your child is being down on himself—"I just can't get this right"—point out (again, gently) that this is new territory for him, so it will be tricky in the beginning but you know he'll get it in time. Firstborns need to know you believe in them and are behind them, but they don't want to be pushed. They're already doing enough pushing of themselves in the area of perfectionism and criticism.

3. *Recognize your firstborn's special place in the family by giving him privileges to go along with the additional responsibilities that come his way.* As he grows older, don't pile on more responsibilities. The other children may be younger, but they're not helpless. They can do

certain duties too. Make sure everyone in the family pulls their weight.

One firstborn told me, "I'm the garbage person." He meant not only that he took out the garbage but that he had to do everything at home while his younger brother and sister got off much easier. So don't build resentment in your firstborn by dumping extra work on him.

4. *Don't treat her as the instant babysitter for the younger children in your family.* When the situation comes up (and it will), check with your firstborn to see if her schedule would allow for some babysitting later that day or in the evening. In other words, don't take your firstborn for granted.

5. *Take time with your firstborn alone.* Do something together that he enjoys, without the younger siblings tagging along. Best-case scenario: have both parents take the child out to do something. Adult company is very important to firstborns because they remember what things were like before siblings came along.

Firstborn Parent with Middleborn Child

Since the middle child's mantra in life is to avoid conflict at all costs, this is the child with whom you'll have the least amount of conflict. Because this child was squeezed between youngest and oldest, she's learned that life often isn't fair, but that's just the breaks. She's an independent thinker who has reasonable expectations of life. She's diplomatic and the peacemaker between her siblings. She has had less of your focused time, so relationships with peers are very important to her. She's a loyal friend, and she knows how to keep secrets.

She's also the one who is the least likely to share her heart or ideas with you.

What does your middleborn need from you?

5 Tips for Parenting a Middleborn

1. *Ask him what he thinks.* Because he's stuck in the middle between the more determined (the oldest) and the more vocal and entertaining (the youngest), he rarely gets to put his two cents in. He needs to know that what he thinks counts.

2. *Let her pick sometimes where the family goes on outings.* The middleborn needs to know that her interests are just as important as the rest of the family's. Otherwise she'll tend to bow to what everyone else wants to do.

3. *Realize how crucial peer relationships are to him.* Go out of your way to include one of his friends on an outing or have some of his friends over after school.

4. *Recognize her position as peacemaker in the family, and thank her for it.* "Caitlyn, I noticed that you helped your brothers come up with a good solution today when they were upset. I appreciate your listening skills, sensitivity, and quick thinking." Then let her know that you don't always expect her to be the one to step in. She doesn't always need to be negotiating between warring parties.

5. *Be sensitive to when he needs help and when he wants to try something on his own.* A middleborn doesn't want to admit when he needs help. He certainly doesn't want help from the older bossy sibling, nor does he want to look like the baby of the family. So he often doesn't receive the help he needs.

Firstborn Parent with Youngest Child

Admit it: by the time baby #3 or #4 is born, you're a little worn down. You're a veteran parent by now. You're much more liable to let things slide with your youngest child. And it's easy to do that with the charming baby of the family. She's the affectionate one, the one everyone loves. She's people oriented and loves being the star of the family show.

The youngest doesn't give up easily, because she knows that her tenacity is usually rewarded. "Mom, can I have that last cookie?" she asks with a smile. You say no a couple times, then wave your hand toward the cookie jar. Another jackpot for the little nipper.

The youngest is the entertainer when your friends come over. "Attention seeker" is her middle name. Although you have high standards and a definite idea of the way life is going to be, your youngest child blows those well-formed, neatly packaged ideas out the window. She's the one, like my grand-daughter, Adeline, who is most likely to walk around with her underwear tucked into her back pocket. Of all your children, she's the hardest to punish because you can't resist her baby blues. She's so likable and fun to be around that even a firstborn like you lets her get away with murder, though you know you shouldn't. Because she's your last child, you cut her some extra slack. (And she's not the only one of your children who notices.)

What does your baby of the family need from you?

5 Tips for Parenting a Baby of the Family

1. *Hold the little charmer accountable to do his chores.* When a job has to be done, don't always call upon the firstborn and the secondborn. Little Schnooky is fully

capable of doing chores that are age appropriate. She needs to pull her weight.

2. *Be aware that she is manipulative by nature, and don't fall for her schemes.* Your thirty-four-pound baby of the family is fully capable of directing you, her parent, to do things you'd ordinarily never do—all with a crook of her little finger, a wheedling tone, or a temper tantrum. Babies of the family have incredibly strong persuasive abilities. (That's why they make great salespeople later on in life.)

3. *Let him learn about consequences.* He may be spontaneous and carefree, but he'll never learn about consequences if you continue to rescue him. Every once in a while, it's okay to let it rain on the baby's parade.

4. *Teach your child that the world isn't all about her.* She is one cog on the wheel of life, not the center of it, and the best time for her to find that out is now. Making her the center of attention is doing her a disservice, as cute as she is.

5. *Teach him about delayed gratification.* A baby wants everything now, but don't give him everything now. (And don't allow his siblings to either.) The adage is true: good things come to those who wait. (And waiting makes babies more patient.)

Two Special Relationships

Within the home are two very special relationships worth noting: the daddy/daughter relationship and the mother/son relationship. Why are these particular relationships so important? Because it's through a daughter's relationship

Match the Person to the Birth Order

Most likely to be stubborn
Most likely to be bossy
The negotiator
Most likely to have a pet name
Most likely to point the finger of blame
Has the most friends
Most likely to say, "I don't care," when
  they really do care
Could charm the socks off an elephant
Least likely to tell you how they feel
Most secretive
Most likely to show off

Firstborn
  (or Only)

Middleborn

Lastborn

See page 281 for the answers.[4]

with her daddy that she develops her view of who males are and how she should relate to them. And it's through a son's relationship with his mother that he develops his view of who females are and how he should treat them.

Daddy and Daughter

A daughter's relationship to her father is the crucial one for her, because that dad represents to her what men are all about.

If Dad is affectionate, loving, and involved, the daughter emerges from her childhood with a strong view of herself—someone worthy to be loved—and a healthy perspective of what relationships with males should be like.

If Dad abandons his daughter emotionally or physically, that daughter is going to develop a good case of male hunger. You don't have to let your imagination wander too far to realize how a girl age 14 to 17 will express male hunger. She will tend to become attached to men quickly, will become sexually active early and outside of marriage, and will be attracted to older men, in order to replace that "daddy figure" missing in her life.

And there are people besides that daughter who will pay for the abandonment by her father. She will be drawn toward guys but also will be like the black widow spider, which eats her mate, to get back at her father. So her father's abandonment sets up an entire negative lifestyle for her—and it affects those she comes in contact with.

Can the cycle be avoided? Yes, with the careful introduction of surrogate males in that young girl's life: a grandfather, an uncle, a good friend of the family, a stepdad. The important thing is that the young woman has a healthy relationship with a man who can be a good daddy figure, who can show her how a lady should be treated, and who can affirm her for the beautiful young lady she's becoming.

The words that a daddy uses with his daughter are also crucial to her development. A sarcastic, critical-eyed dad (as we discussed in chapter 6) will cut a daughter to the quick. Yet a daughter is so fiercely loyal even to an absentee dad that just watch what happens if someone says something negative about him, even if he has left the family—she'll build him into the father of the year. That's because a daughter has a psychological need to invent that relationship if it's not there.

If you've ever been out West, you might have had one of the best burgers ever at the In-N-Out Burger. If we're out driving, my wife—who, like many women, eats more greens than a goat in springtime—will often say, "Ooh, there's an In-N-Out Burger. Flip a U-ey." (I hope the people at In-N-Out Burger appreciate this blatant commercial announcement for their burgers.)

In-N-Out Burgers are incredible. But In-N-Out fathers? The kind of fathers who come and go on their own timetable? The kind of fathers who enter a kid's life when it's convenient for them and then leave? Those kinds of fathers are not good for kids. Quite frankly, a child would be better off without that father in the picture at all than for him to come and go sporadically. As difficult as it is for a child not to have her father involved in her life, an In-N-Out father won't do much for her.

But when a dad expresses confidence in his daughter and reaffirms her femininity, he is investing a great deal in her future. Research says that as goes dad, so goes daughter. A dad affirms his daughter when he comments to her, "Honey, I appreciate the way you take pride in the way you look and dress. You're a beautiful young lady. And you're using your head about parties to go to and not go to, and about guys you're going to date and not date. I'm proud of you."

> Research says that as goes dad, so goes daughter.

A daughter needs to know she is appreciated for who she is and that Dad notices her extra effort in athletics or her pursuit of excellence in the chess club.

Dad, slipping your daughter a commercial announcement—"I appreciate you for who you are"—doesn't cost you a nickel, but it'll have a lifelong effect on that daughter, her husband-to-be, and her children.

Mother and Son

The mother/son relationship is of primary importance in how a young male is going to grow up. Although a young male notices how Dad acts toward Mom, the key parent in a boy's life is Mom. That's why I encourage young moms never to take any mouthiness from their sons.

For centuries, men have wiped their feet on women. They have used women in many ways, and it has to stop. So make sure that you, as a woman, don't take any back talk from little Fletcher. Never let him hit you, even when he's young. If you allow him to do that, it's highly likely that someday he'll enter into a relationship with a woman he can run over. He'll become abusive to her.

How can you take steps so that doesn't happen? From day one, you need to command respect as a mom and a female figure in your home. When you rear your boy with that understanding, you are doing your daughter-in-law a great service. Someday she'll thank you for it.

Encouraging Firstborn Responsibility in *All* Your Children

Your firstborn is the reliable, conscientious list maker, so what do you do? You put her in charge. If you want something done, you call the firstborn. Your middle child will help but often escapes to the back bedroom. And your baby? He finds a way to get big sister to do the work.

Now, I ask you, is this fair to your firstborn?

When you go to the store, what do you do? You tell your firstborn, "Okay, I have to run to the store. You're in charge." And you give the firstborn the job of chief security guard and babysitter. If something goes awry while you're gone, whose fault is it? The firstborn's, of course, because you left her in charge.

I ask you again: is this fair to your firstborn?

If you want responsible children, you teach them to be what? Responsible. So don't do things for your younger children that they can do for themselves. Don't let them slip out of their responsibilities, no matter their birth order or age. Don't allow the firstborn to do more than her share or take over her siblings' workload just because she's better and faster at it.

Hold each of your children—including middleborns and babies—accountable. After all, you're all members of the same family; you should each share in the work and the rewards. Encouraging firstborn responsibility in all your children will go a long way toward your firstborn feeling like a member of the family, rather than simply the lead worker bee.

Equal Treatment = Trouble

Your kids are at it again.

"He did it!" one claims.

"She *made* me," the other fires back.

Sibling rivalry has been around since Cain and Abel. It won't go away. But you can minimize it if you understand what's behind the rivalry: a child's need to be noticed and feel special, and a parent's need "to treat all my kids the same."

For example, you say to Robbie's younger brother, "Do you remember when Robbie did that for the first time?" How does your child interpret your words, even if they were said kindly? "Son, you're number two. Your brother has done that before, so it's no big deal. Nothing special, nothing new." Talk about deflating a kid!

Avoid comparisons at all cost. Consider each child a unique creation.

There's no doubt your kids are different. So why should you treat them the same? The state you live in doesn't treat them the same. A 16-year-old is driving, a 14-year-old is wishing, and a 12-year-old just wants a ride somewhere. Even God Almighty doesn't treat us all the same. He gave us different gifts and temperaments. How boring the world would be if he had made everything "even Stephen." If you insist your kids have to be treated equally, then your 2-year-old will have the same 9:30 bedtime as your 11-year-old. How much sense would that make?

To minimize sibling rivalry, don't get into who started it. Fighting is an act of cooperation. If you don't think so, recall the last disagreement you had with your spouse. What little zingers did you use—words or actions you know really bug your spouse—to escalate the situation?

Fighting always takes two, so both need to be held accountable. Let's say two of your kids are fighting over the last piece of chocolate cake. Give your 10-year-old a knife and say, "Okay, you cut." She'll start to grin, thinking she's won this round. Then turn to the 9-year-old and say, "You get first choice on which piece to take."

Think that would end the debate quickly? You bet.

Winning Relationships

Every child in your family will have their own individual bent. Your firstborn will devour any reading material and seek after excellence. Your secondborn would rather read people; curveballs to him are an adventure. Then there's your baby, who has never met a stranger and will do his own thing.

Your role? To come alongside each of your children, recognize their differences, allow them to take different paths in life, and act as their encourager.

Your children need you to help them face and conquer their problems so they're empowered to make good decisions in the future. They need your affirmation not only of what they do but of who they are. And they need you to enjoy the ride along the way.

8

The Firstborn Advantage at School

> How to use your firstborn nature to set reasonable
> goals and to encourage both yourself and your chil-
> dren as you pursue excellence . . . not frustration.

D o you remember life as a kid? Do you remember walking through that door into kindergarten for the first
time? It was a big world, wasn't it? Do you remember your
parent saying, "Come on, go in. You'll like it." You weren't so
sure. The first few days might not have been so terrific. After
all, you had to share crayons and fat pencils with other kids
who didn't treat them the same way you did. (And you hated
getting the broken ones.)

The playground was another rude awakening. You thought
your little sister was loud at home. But that was nothing
compared to the noise and chaos of the playground. But little
by little, you found friends. And soon you found yourself

organizing games on the playground. Instead of every kid looking around stupidly, wondering what to play and who to play with, they looked to you. "What should we play? Horses or dogs?" So you sealed the deal with just one word, and everyone was off running.

Back in your classroom, you were a great helper, someone Mrs. Smith could always count on to pass out the papers correctly. So you became a leader there as well. For art projects, kids were always craning their necks to see what you were doing, and then they'd copy your idea. But you weren't so crazy about that, because you liked being unique. You got chosen to be the soloist in the kindergarten concert too. (You liked that, except for the dumb leaf hat you had to wear.)

You also discovered how much you thought of books as your friends. After all, you'd been reading since you were 4, and now you discovered chapter books while most of the other kids were still struggling over *Dick and Jane*. You zoomed ahead. You were primed for success. But sometimes, because of that success, you felt a little lonely. Other kids called you "bossy" or "teacher's pet" or "know-it-all."

Do any of these sound familiar?

A Little Competition Never Hurt Anyone, Did It?

Do you know what Baby Einstein is? If you're a parent, I bet you do. Whoever thought Baby Einstein would be given the Nobel Prize for music? Parents love those CDs because every parent (and a firstborn parent in particular) wants their child to be an Einstein.

As soon as a child is born, parents have visions of sugar plums—and great victories for their son or daughter—dancing in their heads. And guess which children are the recipients of the biggest plans? You guessed it: firstborns. They are the trial run for the new parents, after all. And parents (especially firstborn moms) can be terribly competitive.

For example, take this exchange of two moms talking over carrot cake after a Mothers of Preschoolers (MOPS) session. Mom 1 says, "Brittany toilet trained just beautifully at 22 months. It was so easy. . . . How's Jessie doing? She should be trained by now too. She is, right?"

There is a long pause while befuddled Mom 2 thinks of what to say. "Well, we're struggling with that a little bit. We're not there . . . yet."

Mom 1 says, "Isn't she nearly 3?"

Mom 2 lowers her head. "She turned 3 last month."

Mom 1 walks away, thinking, *My kid is sure ahead of your kid.*

Mom 2 walks away, thinking, *I blew it again. What's wrong with me? What's wrong with Jessie? Why isn't it a snap for us?*

Ah, the mom competition. The "let's see who's the head bluebird at the top of the tree" competition.

But the truth is, children toilet train at different ages— when they're ready. Forcing them to be ready won't do either of you any good.

I always tell parents to look at the long view. Do you think your child will still be putting on diapers when she's 15? That's highly unlikely, unless there's a physical problem. And if she's ready to walk through that kindergarten door, do you really think she's going to want to be the only child on the playground who needs to have her diaper changed every couple hours? Wanting to be "a big girl" can be a powerful motivator.

And if your child isn't toilet trained by kindergarten, could it be that she isn't ready for kindergarten and needs another year at home? Would that be such a sin?

All children develop differently. Your responsibility as a parent is to look for readiness in moving from stage to stage.

> All children develop differently. Your responsibility as a parent is to look for readiness in moving from stage to stage.

But firstborn parents in particular are always pushing their firstborn children to succeed early in life. And firstborns are already driven toward success. They often crawl earlier. They walk earlier. They run earlier. They toilet train earlier. Could it be that because they relate more to adults than to other children, they copy adult behavior more quickly? Who wants to crawl for long when they can move at a swift pace with their feet, like Mom and Dad do? Who wants a diaper, a pull-up, or that little potty that sits on the floor when they can have the real deal that Mom and Dad use? That's so much more interesting.

Parents today are driven by competition. They're driven to find a preschool "with strong math and science preparation." But I think there's something wrong with that picture. Isn't preschool about learning to play well with others and enjoying finger painting? Why is it so serious from the start?

If you're a firstborn, you look at all of life—including your child's education—through your own filter of perfection. If your child doesn't get accepted at the "right" preschool, then you jump right to the worry of him not getting into the right college.

That's why you buy educational games that say "appropriate for ages 6–9" and push them on your 4-year-old. Let me tell you, Madison Avenue sure knows how to market to parents. The unwritten message? "Well, parent, of course you don't want your kid to fall behind."

But don't fall into the trap of hurrying your child's education. Your firstborn especially doesn't need to be pushed. He has enough pressure already just from his position on the family tree.

The Family Tree

Think of your family as a tree. The trunk of the tree represents your family. Branches shoot off in all directions—in *different* directions. And once those directions are chosen and established, the branch continues to grow in that direction. If the firstborn has been on his own for three or more years, his branch is growing strongly in the top position. And that branch is likely to keep going. But what if he is only 18 months older than the secondborn? What if the secondborn is more aggressive, more beautiful, or physically larger than the firstborn (as we talked about in chapter 2)? Then the firstborn's branch is more vulnerable to being overtaken. The closer the children in age, the greater the competition, and therefore the greater the possibility of having a role reversal. Add a critical-eyed parent to the mix, and you can nearly guarantee that the secondborn will leap over the firstborn, to the firstborn's detriment.

Think about your own family when you were growing up. What birth order positions did you and your siblings fall into, and why? As the firstborn, did you zoom ahead with firstborn success or become a discouraged perfectionist? What role did your secondborn brother or sister play in the competition game? What role did your parents play?

The Firstborn IQ

Researchers now say that the oldest children in families tend to develop higher IQs than their siblings. "The average difference in I.Q. was slight—three points higher in the eldest child than in the closest sibling—but significant."[1] Why is that? Because that's the difference between a high B average and a low A. And that can have a big effect on which college or university you're accepted into. Interestingly, oldest children scored 4 percent higher in IQ than thirdborns.

The study goes on: "Social scientists have proposed several theories to explain how birth order might affect intelligence scores. Firstborns have their parents' undivided attention as infants, and even if that attention is later divided evenly with a sibling or more, it means that over time they will have more cumulative adult attention, in theory enriching their vocabulary and reasoning abilities."[2]

Could it also have to do with the fact that firstborns, in general, are more disciplined, more responsible, and higher achievers? Laterborn siblings often develop other skills to distinguish themselves, "like social charm, a good curveball, mastery of the electric bass, acting skills."[3]

Is it any surprise that firstborns have won more Nobel Prizes than any other birth order? Can you name the only US president who was a Rhodes Scholar? If you guessed Bill Clinton, you're right.

When it comes to academic excellence, firstborns win across the board.

"Come on now, Dr. Leman," you're saying, "you're really generalizing here."

I'll put up a hundred-dollar bill for every firstborn who is the achiever in their family. Firstborns are the ones who score high on their ACTs. Does that mean we laterborns are relegated to selling newspapers on the street corners? No. But the firstborn is on the success track early in life.

Firstborns also tend to do well in science and math, since they are very logical and analytical. Of the first twenty-three astronauts in space, twenty-one were firstborns and two were "onlies." There wasn't a youngest or a middle in sight. The Mercury Seven astronauts were firstborn sons. In the *Challenger* disaster in 1986, 37-year-old firstborn Christa McAuliffe, married with two children, was to be the first schoolteacher in space. BBC News reported that she'd been picked from among ten thousand entries.[4] Sounds like a firstborn to me.

Is it any surprise that you find firstborns in architecture, engineering, anesthesiology, medicine in general, and any other area where perfection reigns, such as being a concert violinist? I know a firstborn 8-year-old (who is also an only child) who does music theory books for fun. Then there's my firstborn daughter Lauren (there's enough age gap between my children that I have two subfamilies within my family), who looks at her Latin book in the car when I'm taking her to school in the morning.

"Quiz today?" I ask.

"No," she says. "I just thought it would be wise to review my verbs."

Now that would be the last thing on this baby's mind. I was enjoying the morning breeze and some good ol' rock 'n' roll on the radio.

E for Excellence

It's interesting that firstborn comedian Bill Cosby, the oldest of eight children, gave all of his own five children names that started with the letter *E* to remind them to pursue excellence.

Cosby, who holds a doctorate, stands firm on his belief that education and character correction can greatly improve any community. "When a girl says, 'I want to have a baby because I want something that loves me,' we need to talk to her about her idea of love," he says.[5]

Has Cosby's pursuit of excellence always been understood? No. But he remains steadfastly committed to raising the bar in excellence in education—and he isn't letting any naysayers stop him.

You see, it's in the very nature of firstborns to pursue excellence.

Getting Off to School on the Right Foot

Firstborns have a running start from the time the very first school bell rings to "Pomp and Circumstance" at their graduation.

But does that mean you should thrust your firstborn into the competitive world of school as soon as possible? If your child is born late in the school year (say June, July, or August), should you put her in kindergarten as soon as she turns five?

My advice? Don't be so eager to thrust your child into the school environment if she is young. Better to go in as an older child than a younger. The yearlong wait won't kill either of you (as much as your child may want to go to school or as much as you may want her to go), and you'll be paving the way to better success in all areas of her life. Some firstborns may be ready for the academic life, but they may not be ready emotionally for the climate of school, including the chaos, the demands, and the continual social interaction.

School is life's first proving ground, and it can be particularly stressful for the perfectionistic firstborn. Firstborns by nature take things harder than the other birth orders. Disorganization bothers them. They are driven to get the work done, often before it's due, so they naturally up the ante on themselves. They can't just draw a simple picture; they have to spend two hours on it to get it perfect. They're often found curled up with a book, restudying what they've just studied to make sure they've gotten it right.

> Children need to be children as long as possible.

With their birth order and their continued drive to succeed, firstborns win. But at what cost?

Children need to be children as long as possible. Soon enough they'll be paying bills like the rest of us. One of your biggest jobs as the parent of a firstborn is to watch the stress and pressure level in your child. Firstborns will always take life seriously. Sometimes they need to lighten up. Getting a B- in gym isn't the end of the world. And just because a picture doesn't end up the way your child wants it to doesn't mean it should get ripped up in frustration and thrown in the trash.

Perfect Child in an Imperfect World

Because firstborns are structured, organized, self-disciplined, analytical, and logical, they just know the way things ought

193

to be. In fact, they can see the "perfect" picture in their head: what the art project ought to look like, what score they ought to get on a math test, how the school musical should be run, how to run the bases to get a home run. . . .

But what happens when perfection doesn't meet real life? The firstborn can become discouraged and think, *This isn't the way it's supposed to be.* Over time, this can lead to a discouraged perfectionist who no longer wants to try for fear of failing—like the firstborn who finishes all his homework but then doesn't give it to the teacher to grade. *What if I don't get a perfect score?* he thinks. *It's better not to turn it in than to risk that.*

A healthy imagination is good for firstborns. There's nothing at all wrong with daydreaming—as long as it doesn't control their lives. But firstborns can get themselves in trouble when the fantasy in their head (remember, they're bred for perfection) is much stronger than reality. Be honest with your child. Tell her that sometimes she'll succeed at a task; sometimes she'll fail.

Do you as a firstborn get down on yourself when you fail and tell yourself you'll never amount to anything? If so, take a look at this list of influential people who didn't get straight A's:

Charles Darwin, who did not do well in school as a child and failed a university medical course

Albert Einstein, who performed poorly in almost all of his high school courses and flunked his college entrance exams

Sir Winston Churchill, who was at the bottom of his class in one school and failed the entrance exam to another

Pablo Picasso, who was barely able to read or write at the age
of 10 when his father yanked him out of school; a tutor who
was hired to instruct him gave up and quit in disgust

Paul Ehrlich, the winner of the 1908 Nobel Prize for medicine, who was a poor student who hated exams and could
not give oral presentations or write compositions[6]

What does all of this mean to firstborns? You are in some
mighty good company when you miss
the mark every now and then. Failure
isn't the end of the world, nor is it a
sign that you won't be capable of going
on to do other things.

> The only way to
> avoid failure is
> to sit in a corner
> and do nothing.

What if Louis Pasteur had decided,
because he wasn't the top student in
his chemistry class, that he just wasn't
cut out for this science business, and then opted for another
career?

What if Beethoven's teacher, who called him a "hopeless
dunce,"[7] had been able to convince him of his own worthless-
ness? What if the genius had become so discouraged that he
never composed a note? What a loss that would have been
to all of us.

Let's be blunt. Every human being, including you, who has
ever tried to do anything has failed at one time or another.
And you'll fail again. I don't care how intelligent, talented,
or skilled you are. The only way to avoid failure is to sit in a
corner and do nothing.

But here's the key. When you *do* fail at something, how do
you respond? Do you let that failure defeat you, incapacitate
you, and hold you back from trying again? Or do you see it
as a learning experience?

Model for your children a healthy response to failure—both your own and theirs. If you do, they can move confidently into their future, realizing that failures are merely learning experiences . . . not the end of the world.

The Comparison Game

Firstborns are particularly good at the comparison game.

> *Wow, she's really got it together. Head of the chess club and prom queen. How'd she manage that?*
>
> *That's his third touchdown this game. I only made two last game.*
>
> *Everything comes naturally to her.*
>
> *How'd he get first-chair trumpet?*
>
> *I studied so hard. Why did she get an A?*
>
> *If only I was more like her.*
>
> *If only I was more like him.*

Comparison games don't stop when you're grown up. With firstborns, they can intensify.

Perhaps you compare yourself with the woman across the street: *My! Four beautiful children, and all well behaved. A husband who seems to adore her. Beautiful clothes and a great figure too. Bet she always has dinner with all the food groups on the table. How she finds time to do charity work, run a florist business, and still look that good and put together, I have no idea. . . . Then there's me.*

Or maybe you compare yourself to a co-worker. *Oh, yeah, VP of the bank. Drives that brand-new BMW. Maybe I'll have one someday. He's a tennis champ at that exclusive club too.*

Always surrounded by gorgeous women. Now, if that were me . . .

But what you don't see is that the woman across the street cries every night in bed because she's alone and trapped in a loveless marriage.

And what you don't see is the VP of the bank popping Valium and chugging gin and tonic to ease his mind after another day of heart-stopping pressure on the job.

If you play the comparison game, you no sooner get to one plateau than you set your sights on another. You're on a roller coaster that never ends. Aren't you exhausted? Do you really like life that way? You're rarely able to stop and savor the sweet smell of success, because you always see someone just ahead who is more successful than you are. And your firstborn nature just drives you to catch up.

> If you play the comparison game, you no sooner get to one plateau than you set your sights on another. You're on a roller coaster that never ends.

You're not doing yourself any favors by comparing yourself with others. There are millions of people who are better off in some ways than you are. They may be richer, better-looking, more successful, or more intelligent. And then there are millions who couldn't even begin to compete with you in those areas.

Instead of playing the comparison game, why not focus instead on being the best *you* can be? Use the talents God Almighty gave you. Use your natural firstborn advantage. Why worry about everyone else? And is it really your business anyway? If you're a pursuer of excellence, you're looking ahead with anticipation to see how you can do something better next time. Your eye is on yourself and your skills—not the other person.

Strengths and Weaknesses

You as the parent are in the best position to know your child's strengths and weaknesses better than anyone else. Is your child musically talented? Athletically talented? Does she excel in just about everything related to academics but struggle with making friends?

Parents of firstborns often ask me whether they should seek to put their children in a gifted program. We had our firstborn daughter, Holly, in a gifted program for a while, then took her out. It was over the top, in our opinion, for what could be expected for any child her age.

The goal of any schooling is to encourage a child to think, discover, and grow. You certainly don't want him bored. A lot of children who are bright are bored in school because so many things have been dumbed down to "average" or "below average." If that's the case for your child's school, and your child is showing symptoms of boredom, talk to the teacher. See if he or she can give additional work. (Notice that I didn't say *busywork*—doing five worksheets with the same principle instead of the one everyone else does.) If the teacher is open to that, wonderful. If not, check out after-school programs that would provide enrichment and stimulation, or check into other schools that might better fit your child's needs.

No school will be perfect. But being slightly bored is quite different than your child being pushed to a state of frustration because he can't keep up with impossible demands.

198

There's a wonderful movie called *The Three Amigos*. It's my absolute favorite movie of all time. In the movie, one of the main characters, El Guapo (which means "the handsome one"; ironically, he's very ugly in this movie), says to his gang of outlaws, "I know each of you like I know my own smell."

You, parent, know each of your children the same way. And their schooling is your judgment call. Some firstborns flourish in being homeschooled, some flourish in public schools, and some flourish in private schools. Your job is to make the absolute best choice you can, based on your child's strengths and weaknesses, and then ride the waves with her. Sometimes you'll have to rescue her from the choppy waters; other times you'll need to let her swim for herself.

Your job as a parent isn't to smooth all of the waters of life for your children. They *need* to experience failure. It will make them better people, better husbands and wives, and better daddies and mommies.

Since you're a firstborn, you can identify with the pressures a firstborn feels. You've been there too. That's why, in your own striving for excellence, you have to be careful of pushing your child too hard. Knowing your own tendency to overdo things, how can you be careful not to overdo it with your firstborn?

The Homework Battle

This is one of the biggest areas that parents ask me about. I often hear, "Dr. Leman, it's a fight every night to get Kelsey to do her homework. It about wears me out. And it starts the instant I pick her up from school. I've tried everything, and nothing seems to work. I'm worn out by the end of the evening, my husband is ticked off, my daughter's in tears, and the homework's still not done. . . ."

Let me ask you one question: whose homework is it?

Ah, now we're getting somewhere. As a firstborn, you desperately want your child to succeed. But at what cost to you? Your daughter? Your entire family?

If your home has become a homework battle zone, here are some tips that will help.

1. Remember whose homework it is. Don't do homework for your child—ever.

"I just know I'm going to flunk my math test tomorrow," your firstborn worries out loud. "I don't understand this stuff, and no one will help me."

> Let me ask you one question: whose homework is it?

"Oh, don't you worry. Mommy will help you. We'll work until midnight tonight if we have to, and I'll get you ready for that test."

Never mind that your firstborn has had two weeks to prepare for the test and could have told you or the teacher several days ago if he was having trouble. Whose fault is it that he may flunk? Certainly not yours. As a matter of fact, let's lay blame right where it should be. It's your firstborn's fault.

But when he says that there's no one to help him, he makes *you* feel guilty, so you sit down and spend hours working with him—time you really need to spend doing something else.

My advice? Let the kid flunk the test. Next time he'll be quicker to ask questions when he's having difficulty understanding something.

You are not responsible for your child's bad grade or for his inability to ask questions, get the homework done, or study for the test. Having a compassionate heart is wonderful, but you don't want to teach your child to be an emotional leech, do you?

This is a common scene in households across America. A child will begin his homework, then fuss, "I just don't get it." The parent's response? "Oh, I'll explain it to you."

So the parent explains (but most often the child isn't listening because he's used to the parent doing the work for him, or he simply doesn't want to do the homework), and the child still doesn't seem to get it. So the parent explains again, in a slightly louder, more exasperated tone. The cycle continues until, before long, the other parent (or an older brother or sister) comes to help, adding in their two cents. By now, the child is aggravated more because all he wants is just to be done and go out and play. Before long, everyone in the family is mad at each other. Doors slam. And everyone has a bad rest of the evening. All over homework?

I'm telling you, don't go there. It's not your homework. If your son needs extra help, ask his teacher. If the teacher doesn't have time to help, ask a student in a higher grade (for example, a high school student) to do some tutoring in your home, under your supervision.

Unless you're set up for homeschooling, don't turn your home into a schoolroom. And if you are homeschooling, remember that even the teacher goes home at night and gets a rest from school. The schoolroom should be open only during your regular school day. Would you call a public school teacher at night to ask her about an assignment? Well, then, your children shouldn't ask you either.

Do not do your child's homework—ever. It's his homework; it's his responsibility. Don't rescue him from that if you want a responsible child who will become a responsible adult. And isn't that one of the main goals of parenting?

2. Set aside a specific time—and a specific amount of time—for doing homework.

When does your child usually do homework? She needs a set time in which she's expected to get her homework done. Right after school usually doesn't work. Your child has just spent the majority of the day in intense thought at school. If she walks in the door and you have a homework table set up for her, you're going to begin a battle that will only escalate. Every child, no matter the age, needs time to play or unwind. And firstborns and only children in particular need some alone time to regroup after all the chaos and social interaction they get at school.

So give your child a break. Let her play for a while first. And a snack in the car on the way home always helps everyone's moods—yours included, because you don't have to listen to any whining or complaining. Your child's mouth is too full to engage in it.

An important note here: going to an activity after school (soccer, play rehearsal, music lessons, etc.) is not considered a break for the child. Parents who keep their child involved in too many activities will pay the price—they'll have an exhausted child who is too tired and frazzled to do her homework once she finally does get home. (The Leman rule was always one extra activity per child per semester—no more than that.)

If your family has dinner at a reasonable hour, have your child do her homework after dinner. That will give her the break she needs, everyone's tummies will be full (which helps family harmony and patience), and you'll be more patient with interruptions (if they do come) because you're doing "nonthinking" work like cleaning up the table and doing the dishes.

Also, set a specific amount of time for doing homework. Firstborns are so perfectionistic that they will often go the extra mile to make their work perfect. This isn't a bad thing in itself, but homework can take over your whole evening if your 10-year-old takes a short essay he's supposed to write and then illustrate with a picture, and turns it into a ten-page essay with a Picasso drawing attached. Firstborns need to know that they won't always have the time to do everything they want to do perfectly. Sometimes they just need to get it done.

One mom solved the problem with her fourth-grade perfectionistic firstborn by telling her, "Emily, if you want to do more on that drawing over the weekend when you've got time, great. That would be wonderful. But for now, you've got twenty minutes to get whatever you can done, and then it's bedtime." It worked. And you know what? By the weekend, Emily had forgotten all about the drawing that she'd considered "half finished" (but was miles ahead of anyone else's chicken scratching).

3. Provide a study-friendly environment and the right tools.

Every child needs a friendly environment in which to study. Figure out, with your child, the best environment for homework. If your child is a procrastinator (and discouraged perfectionists can be), doing homework in his bedroom probably isn't a good idea. Yet doing homework in the family room, where little brothers and sisters are running around playing hide-and-seek, isn't the best option either. If you have several children, establish a "quiet hour," and have the children do their work at the dining room or kitchen table. Or your den is another good option. That way you can be within eyesight to make sure no shenanigans are going on.

Also, make sure pencils are sharpened, paper is available, and rulers, calculators, and whatever else your children need for their homework are right within reach. Then children don't have the excuse of going to look for an item instead of finishing their homework.

If the homework involves a computer, make sure the computer is in a high-traffic area of the house. Too many children have been unwittingly introduced to pornography through researching for school projects on the Internet. I suggest that you get some kind of parental control on your Internet service and that you check the history button to see the sites your child is viewing. It also helps to have the screen angled so it's easily visible to you (and anyone else) as they walk through the room.

4. Encourage, but don't hover.

When children are young, you are necessarily more involved. You're the one finding art paper, crayons, etc., that have somehow disappeared into the cracks of the couch. And younger children always want to show you their drawings. That's important to them, so it should be important to you to take a look (even if you can't distinguish exactly what the drawing is). "I bet you had fun drawing that," you can say. And then that little chest will puff out with the joy of accomplishment. You may also need to be actively participating in some situations (for example, it might not be best to have a kindergartner using your heavy-duty stapler or hot-glue gun all by herself).

As your children get older, you can remain in the encouraging role, but your participation should change. You can be available if they have questions, but you shouldn't hover. Your children should know that if they need some help, they can ask you. But they also need to know that you aren't going to do their work for them.

Today's parents tend to go one way or the other: either doing so much of the child's homework that he just waits for them to do it and takes no pride in it, or totally ignoring the child's homework so he feels completely on his own with no support network. The balance is in the middle. Your firstborn needs to know you expect him to do his best. Does that mean he gets a perfect score every time? No. But he does his best.

Your job is to respond to the effort your son or daughter has made. "Wow. You got an A-. You must feel proud of yourself. That was a big project."

Your role is not to be the homework gestapo. It's to encourage your children in the work *they* are doing.

My wife, Sande, and I have five children. Three of them have firstborn personalities (Holly, Kevin II, and Lauren) by ordinal or functional birth order. We have never overdone anything with school or hovered over their homework. (In fact, Lauren is now a freshman in high school, and I don't think I've seen one of her homework papers in years.) Yet all of our children have excelled in school. They know we expect

> Your role is not to be the homework gestapo. It's to encourage your children in the work *they* are doing.

them to give their best. And they do. Is it always perfect? No, but it's their best.

When You Need to Fight the Battle

Many parents get overinvolved at school, trying to fight every little battle for their child.

"How could that little boy be so mean to my son? I need to talk to the teacher about that."

"What was that teacher doing, letting them finger paint all over their desks? My daughter's shirt is ruined."

"I can't believe the playground monitor let the kids splash in the puddles. Little Johnny's socks were wet all day."

I want to be clear here. There are times when you have to let things go if they're not important in the long view of life. You can't major on every minor.

4 Ways to End the Homework Battle

1. Remember whose homework it is. Don't do homework for your child—ever. Get a tutor if needed. A high school or college student will suffice. Find a student close to your neighborhood or one who goes to your church. That way you stay out of the surrogate teacher battle.
2. Set aside a specific time—and a specific amount of time—for doing homework.
3. Provide a study-friendly environment and the right tools.
4. Encourage, but don't hover. Don't be the homework gestapo.

But there are also times when you should get involved at school. When you should ask questions and intervene on behalf of your child.

A firstborn mom approached me a few weeks back. "My son is continually being bullied at school. I'm not sure what to do about it. I want him to be strong and stand up for himself so people don't consider him a wuss, but . . ."

Her son was in second grade; the bully was in seventh grade. That single mom had grown up in a smaller town and in a gentler age, in which the philosophy of her dad was, "If a bully goes after you, hit him back. And then he'll stop." But she was nervous about telling her son to do that, since the bully outweighed him by two and a half times.

"You're right to be nervous," I told her. "You should be. The traditional advice about standing up to a bully doesn't work anymore." I went on to explain how dramatically things have changed in past years. When I grew up, the bully was the kid who followed another kid home from school, taunted him, and maybe pushed him and gave him a bloody nose. Today's bullies carry knives and guns and are a lot more lethal.

If your child is being bullied, you need to go immediately to the teacher and fill her in on the situation. If she doesn't seem concerned, go to the principal. Bullies are serious business, so don't take bullying lightly. It must stop. Now.

And if your child is the bully, the same thing holds true. The bullying must stop. Now.

Upon finding out that her son was bullying a girl in his class, a distraught mom called me. "Dr. Leman, what do I do?"

I gave her this advice: "Tell your son, 'I'm sorry that you feel so bad about yourself that you have to pick on someone else to make you feel better. Let's talk about that.'"

The woman told her son that, and it worked. Her son was stunned and embarrassed that that's how people thought of bullies. He was properly humbled. Accompanied by his mother, he went and apologized to both the girl and her mother.

Bravo to that mom, I say. As embarrassing as that situation was, she took the bull by the horns and brought about a change not only in her son's behavior but in his attitudes about life. That boy will think twice before he bullies another child again.

Another time to be watchful is when your child repeatedly makes comments about a teacher being unfair. You have to be very careful here, since many of these comments have to do with perspective. But there have been occasions where parents have told me about these types of situations:

A third grade teacher routinely assigned nineteen worksheets of math and science homework each week, on top of other homework. (Frankly, no 8- or 9-year-old should be spending three to four hours a night on homework.) I suggested those parents talk to the teacher about her expectations and theirs.

A high school teacher grabbed a girl's arm because she was talking to a friend and didn't see that he had started class. The problem? Not only did the girl get in trouble, but the teacher gripped her so hard he left bruise marks on her arm. Should the girl have been talking? No, that was her fault for not paying attention. But that teacher also had no right to respond in the way he did. He needed to be confronted immediately with the evidence of his action. I told the parents that if the teacher did not respond well or apologize, they should go to the principal and present their case. There's no room for an abusive teacher in a school system.

Heidi, a junior higher, was put on the "unacceptable" list by a group of "cool" junior high girls. Her friends were told that they'd be put on the list too if they kept hanging out with Heidi. Heidi was so harassed that her grades dropped, she lost weight, and she became listless. Because her school was a private school, and the group of "cool" girls came from families that supported the school with large financial donations, the teacher and the principal were unwilling to confront the bully girls and their parents. As a result, Heidi's parents pulled her from that school, and she was home-schooled for a year before going into high school at a completely different location. There are times when you should stick with a school and see it through to the end, and then there are times when your child needs you to enter her world and take charge. This was one of those times.

These are extreme situations, but I mention them because they do exist, and parents are sometimes confronted with them. But on average, many of the battles fought at school are smaller ones, and your child needs to learn how to fight them. Often your firstborn doesn't need your interference; she needs your loving encouragement and belief that she can do it—she can overcome the obstacles she faces each day. Then she has the ingredients she needs to be a confident adult who can take on and solve her own problems.

Encouraging Your Firstborn

What does your child need from you? First of all, firstborns don't need to be motivated. They already have a healthy dose of self-motivation. But what they do need is your *encouragement*. Let me clarify. Encouragement does not mean hovering. No child likes Mom and Dad hovering over their homework to make sure it gets done. Firstborns don't need you to hover; they don't need you to correct their homework. They need you to encourage them as they go ahead. There's a big difference between encouragement ("Wendy, that's a tough concept to get in math, and you nailed it. You must be proud of yourself") and praise ("Oh, Wendy, you're so brilliant. I just knew you could figure that out, and you did. You're such a smart girl!"). Firstborns know that praise is false, so they'll discard it anyway.

They also need your *interest*. "I see you're reading *Sarah, Plain and Tall*. I remember reading that book in fourth grade too. What do you think of it?" Since books are a firstborn's best friend, use this interest as a good discussion tool. It will unwittingly reveal how your firstborn is feeling about their own life and life in general.

They need to be *held responsible*. Their homework is their responsibility. Their practice for the upcoming band competition or soccer tryout is their responsibility. Don't let these things become a battle, and don't take ownership of them.

They need you to *lighten up*. Any child who is pushed will become contrary. Firstborns, if they aren't discouraged perfectionists, have enough motivation to get homework done without a commandant looking over their shoulder. So let them be in charge. Don't overdo the pressure. Flash back to your own childhood. How did *you* feel when Mom or Dad pushed you to do your homework?

They need to know how to *strive for excellence, not perfection*. Firstborns are primed to do everything perfectly. But we don't live in a perfect world. Failure is a part of life. The sooner your children learn that, the better. Failure is not the end of the world. Tell your children about your own failures and what you learned from them. Children see parents as so perfect. If you let your own imperfections show, your children will think, *Okay, so I blew it. Mom and Dad have too. I guess it's not so bad. I don't like it, but life does go on. Now I know what to do next time.*

Going Back to School as an Adult

If you're considering cracking the books yourself, or you're already in a night class or pursuing a degree, I applaud you. You're following your dreams. Good for you. Many of you might have pursued a degree for a couple of years, then you fell in love, got married, and had a couple kids, and now you're back on the hunt to finish your degree. You've discovered that you won't break through that rebarred ceiling without the ticket, and that ticket is a college degree (or a master's or a PhD, depending on your area of interest).

Good news! As a firstborn, you already have an advantage over everyone else. You're disciplined, organized, and analytical, and you naturally rise to the challenge of academia.

The patterns you've built as a firstborn will pay off as you do college and postgrad work, because that work requires behavioral and mental discipline. You'll have to give your best effort. Firstborns thrive in school, the proving ground of life. They find themselves on top in nearly every academic situation because it's a place where they're comfortable. It's

211

easy to know what's expected in school—everything is written down for you in black and white in the curriculum.

It's when firstborn adults step out of school and into real life that they have problems. You might be brighter than bright and have an MBA in business or have grown up in a family business, but can you lead people? Are you a cold fish, or are you dialed in to the needs of others around you?

You might be in engineering school because you're very precise and have tons of ideas for new products. But once you've created an ingenious product, who will find people to sell it for you? Who will organize that sales force? And who will actually market and sell the part? I've got news for you. These people won't be firstborns like you. The middleborns will be the organizers, the worker bees who help you get the job done and find the right people to get it done. The babies—the guys and gals who got through college academics by the skin of their teeth—are the ones who will sell that product for you.

Firstborns tend to be the ones who work their way up the ranks to CEO or the ones who are born into a family business. They tend to be more conservative, following the status quo. Risk taking is not a firstborn character trait. Interestingly, middleborns, such as Bill Gates (who left Harvard to start a little company) or Donald Trump, tend to be more entrepreneurial. They're more likely to roll the dice and gamble on a venture (something a firstborn isn't likely to do).

Again, it all comes down to the fact that every birth order is needed.

You can be a genius, but you won't get far in life without balance.

> You can be a genius, but you won't get far in life without balance.

What If I Bite Off More Than I Can Chew?

I'll use *The Three Amigos* once again. Do you know your own "smell"? Do you know your strengths and weaknesses? How well do you do when you have three irons in the fire at the same time?

In a day when so many adults are getting master's degrees online, firstborns tend to bite off more than they can chew, so they decrease their probability of success. They can look successful from the outside, but on the inside they feel like a failure. Is that you?

Most people—especially perfectionistic firstborns—function better when they do one project at a time, have one commitment at a time, take one class at a time. If you're going back to school, you will need to limit

> How well do you do when you have three irons in the fire at the same time?

your other involvements, such as volunteering at school, at your place of faith, or in your community, or working overtime hours at work. We all have our limits. And as important as school and work are, you need time to enjoy other things, such as spouse, children, friends, and free time.

You know yourself best. Is now the time to pursue a degree? If so, go for it. Just realize that your life priorities and calendar will need to be adjusted.

The Furious Charge

Do you like to put off your schoolwork until the end of the week and then do the "furious charge" to get it done? And then does everyone in the family pay for it?

213

What can you learn about tackling that project in a more precise manner and in doable increments? Perhaps you should spend a couple hours every night after the kids are in bed to work on it—instead of having the whole family on pins and needles and tiptoeing around on eggshells while you hit the ground running on Saturday morning and try to get the project done by your Monday night class.

> **Going Back to School**
>
> **4 Ways to Make It a Winning Proposition**
> 1. Take only one class at a time.
> 2. Rearrange your schedule; limit volunteer work and overtime.
> 3. Avoid the "furious charge" to get your homework done.
> 4. Welcome the input of respected mentors.

You're organized by nature, so why not use your firstborn advantage? You're disciplined by nature, so put that to work too. Create limits for your homework time and for your expectations. If you're married, sit down and do this with your spouse. Then take a relational risk (something that's hard for firstborns) and say, "Honey, I want you to keep me accountable for this. I want to work two hours every night on this project. I'm asking you to help me. If I turn on the TV after the kids go to bed, will you gently remind me I need to keep my promise? And if I'm still working past the two hours, would you let me know my time's up?"

This way you, by nature a solo kind of person, are involving someone else in your decision. You need accountability to keep you on track and to keep your life in balance, since you as a firstborn can be an all-or-nothing kind of person.

And one more thing: when you tell your spouse, "I welcome your input," don't say it unless you really mean it.

5 Ways to Cut Yourself
—and Your Firstborn—
Some Slack

1. *See your failures as setbacks, not fatal errors.* (So you got a C in chemistry. That doesn't mean you're a failure as a human being.)

   Learn from your failures. They're not the enemy.

2. *Take a realistic look at yourself and your talents.* Strive for excellence, not perfection. (Just because you didn't make the basketball team doesn't mean you couldn't still work on your skills and play with the guys for fun. And just because you didn't nail the quote for the top client this time doesn't mean you won't next time.)

3. *Learn to live in the real world, where people are imperfect and things just happen.* (Like when you have a pop quiz the one time you haven't studied.)

4. *Face up to your fears.* (The teacher you fear brushes her teeth, just like you do. The boss may not be as intimidating as he looks. Maybe he just needs a course on how to communicate.)

5. *Take responsibility for your actions.* (If you didn't get the paper done on time, don't tell the teacher your dog ate it—you'd have to do the paper in order for the dog to eat it. If you were supposed to round up speakers for a seminar and you dropped the ball, you'd best admit it now.)

   To throw up your hands and say, "I just *knew* this was going to happen; it *always* happens to me!" doesn't help much, does it? But what if you looked instead at the situation and what caused you to fail? Then you could say, "Okay, I see where I went wrong this time. Now that I understand the project better, I won't make the same mistake next time." Ah, now that's progress. And isn't that what school is all about?

Facing Your Fears

We all are afraid of something.

I don't care if you're tougher than Rambo or Indiana Jones; there are still things that cause your pulse to quicken and the hair on the back of your neck to stand up.

Like speaking in public, for one. That's a common fear.

But guess what? If you deny your fear, you're not gaining anything. You can't overcome your fears unless you face up to them and, in a sense, learn to accept them.

Let's say you are afraid to speak in public. When you enter a school environment, you will, no doubt, have to make presentations. So what should you say to yourself?

"I feel afraid because I'm going to have to give a speech in front of the entire class. I'm not really accustomed to public speaking, so it's only normal that I would feel a little nervous."

Now, what's the worst thing that could happen? Would that kill you?

"But what if I forgot my speech or said something stupid, and everyone laughed at me?"

And would that be the end of the world? If you analyze your fears, you take the first step in conquering them.

"Okay, so I'm afraid, but what could really happen?"

Why not make light of your fear, such as starting off your speech with a joke about having to shout to make yourself heard above the knocking of your knees? That would make your audience laugh, and laughter eases fear.

Why not learn to admit when you're afraid? Everyone is afraid at one time or another. Then show that you can laugh about your fears. Life can go on, in spite of you having to do what you don't necessarily want to do.

216

Don't let fear paralyze you from stepping ahead confidently into your dreams. I love hearing about 80-year-olds who go back to school to pursue a college degree or take art, photography, or writing classes. The cement of an 80-year-old's life is not only well-formed; it's cracking a little bit. But isn't it nice to know that an 80-year-old can still make an impression? My hat is off to such people.

"I'm a Winner!"

Years ago I taught behaviorally disturbed children. These kids were nasty to each other in every way, and when I say nasty, I mean nasty. I had to teach them P.E., among other things. There was no gym at the mental health center, so we used the local Y.

There we played all sorts of games, but every game seemed to turn brutal, especially for one little boy named Richie. We'd play battle ball with a rubber ball, and the idea was to tag someone with the ball. Poor Richie was so wide he was almost a square, so he made a great target. Balls would go flying in his direction and nearly pound him to pieces. I felt really sorry for him. I've always been the kind of person who looks for the best in people and accentuates the positives, but in Richie's case, I was stymied.

One day the solution hit me. "Okay," I said, "everyone on the floor. Now."

The kids just stared at me. "What do you mean?"

"I mean, on the floor—now," I stated.

Slowly they got down on the floor on their knees. I saw them giving each other the eye. They knew I was different

217

from the average bear, but where was this going? I could see the questions in their eyes.

Then I said, "Lay down on the floor."

And so the boys did. Except for Richie, who was still in a squat position, trying to lower himself to the floor.

"We're going to have a rolling contest," I said. "We're going to roll from this end of the gym to the other wall and back."

The first couple times we tried this, I saw the potential in Richie. So I showed him how to put his arms out straight above his head so he could roll more quickly.

The kid got it, and he started to roll. I mean, he *really* started to roll. And he could roll fast. Just imagine a big root beer barrel dropping down a mountainside and rolling at top speed.

Guess what? Richie beat everyone by yards. The first time he won, his response was breathtaking. I'll never forget it.

Richie struggled to his knees, then up to his feet. Then, with arms stretched above his head, he clenched his fists and yelled out, "I'm a winner! I'm a winner! I won! I won!" His voice rang out across that gym.

You see, everyone—firstborns included—wants to be a winner. You do, and so does your child. The trick is identifying your strengths, improving your weaknesses, facing your fears, welcoming others' input, and then going for it.

You never know what you can do until you try.

9

The Firstborn Advantage at Work

How you can win at business anytime and all the time.

L et's say you're in someone's office. You notice that the pictures are hung perfectly, the office is spotless, and the few piles on the desk are in pristine order. A sweater or jacket hangs neatly over the back of the desk chair. What would you guess about that person's birth order?

Hands down, that person is a firstborn. Babies of the family tend to have clutter and piles they ignore. (They hope the perfectionistic firstborn will come along, see the piles, and organize the mess for them.) Firstborns have a need for power and control. They need things to be orderly. They're disciplined, go-for-the-goal kind of people. They're analytical and logical, they're smarter than the average bear, and they get things done. No matter the task, you can count on the firstborn.

Firstborns are indeed the movers and shakers of the world. They also appear in greater numbers than their siblings in *Who's Who in America* and *American Men and Women of Science*, as well as among the ranks of Rhodes Scholars and college professors.

Ben Dattner, a psychology professor at New York University who has studied birth order, says it makes sense that firstborn children rise to the top: "They are more extroverted, confident, assertive, authoritarian, dominant, inflexible, conformist, politically conservative, task oriented, conscientious, disciplined, defensive about errors, and fearful of losing position or rank."[1]

In the seminars I conduct for corporate executives, I always conduct a survey to find out how many are firstborns. In the last two groups I spoke to, here's what I found, and it squares with every other group I've talked to over the years: in a seminar for chief executive officers, nineteen of the twenty attending were firstborns. In a seminar for young presidents, twenty-three of the twenty-six dynamic young men and women were firstborns.

As mentioned earlier, firstborns have also won more Nobel Prizes in science than laterborns, "but often by advancing current understanding, rather than overturning it."[2] Frank Sulloway, a research scholar at MIT, "spent twenty-six years accumulating massive statistical evidence to show that there is a real difference between first borns, who tend to be conservative and stick with the status quo, and later borns, who are more open-minded and willing to take risks and explode cherished ideas and theories."[3] Sulloway gave a reason for this:

Openness to experience—first borns are more conforming, traditional, and closely identified with parents.

Conscientiousness—first borns are more responsible, achievement oriented, organized, and planful.

Extraversion—first borns are more extraverted, assertive, and likely to exhibit leadership.[4]

In other words, if you want something done properly, get a firstborn to do it. No wonder so many firstborns are doctors, lawyers, and engineers. They sit on school boards, on city councils, and in the United States Congress.

USA Today reports:

> Why do firstborn children so dominate the boardroom? CEOs themselves say they got hit in the face early in life with a stew of factors. Those included the undivided attention, at least for a time, from their parents. They say they felt the pressure of greater expectations. They were forced to become self-sufficient because they had to look after younger siblings while not having an older sibling looking out for them.[5]

Many firstborns may be geniuses. They may be top dogs at their company or in their community. They may excel at academia. But many of them don't do well in life. Why is that? Because they lack balance.

Firstborns seem to come in two varieties. Either they are the workers who take on everyone else's work as well as their own (someone has to do it, they reason, and they can get it done, and get it done right), or they end up being dictators who use or run over anyone in their path.

But the ones who have learned to use their firstborn character traits to their own advantage and everyone else's—what wonders they can accomplish! Even better, those firstborns will bring a whole team along with them—a team that trusts and supports them and feels good about the mission of the company.

Whether you work in an office, a plane hangar, or a home business, or you're rounding up volunteers for a charity affair, you too can develop a supportive team if you follow the principles in this chapter.

Are You Too Responsible?

You're good at what you do. You're efficient. You always follow through. It's no wonder your co-workers naturally look to you to take charge (translation: to do the dirty work that they don't want to do).

Take Jana, a part-time nurse who was always cleaning up the kitchen at the pediatrician's office. Even though it was no one's assigned job, she'd clean the refrigerator on Friday and leave it sparkling clean, then come back on Tuesday and find that it was just as gross as always. After reading *The Birth Order Book*, she got suspicious, so she did some investigating. Guess what? The other three women in the office were all youngest daughters, and their daily mantra was, "Someone will be there to pick up after me. Mom always did." So guess who stopped being Mom? (Even though she did have to avoid the fridge for a few weeks before her co-workers got a clue. There's something about food growing green and blue mold that does the trick.)

Every firstborn does battle with this pesky thought: *If I don't do it, it won't get done . . . or it won't get done right.* So you, of course, feel led to take the matter into your own hands. Then

Match the Occupation with Birth Order

	Anesthesiologist
	Super salesman (could sell dead rats for a living)
	Comedian
	Pharmacist
	Social worker
	Interior designer
	Architect
Firstborn	Math teacher
(or Only)	Watchmaker/jeweler
	English teacher
Middleborn	General sales manager
Lastborn	Manager
	P.E. teacher
	CEO
	Diplomat
	Electrician
	Recreational therapist
	Nurse
	Attorney
	Social studies teacher

See page 282 for the answers.[6]

what happens? You get one task, then another, then another . . . and soon it's a whole lot to do.

The next time you're approached to do a task, or that inner voice prompts you to do something, try these steps first.

1. Practice saying no.

If you're not used to saying no, practice doing so. You can be polite and friendly and still say no in a firm way that leaves no doubts about your position. If you're always called upon to take charge, you'll do yourself a tremendous favor if you learn to say:

> "I'll have to say no to that, because I really don't have the time."
>
> "I appreciate your asking me, but I'm going to say no this time."
>
> "I'm sorry, but I can't possibly take on any more projects right now."

Even a simple "Thank you for asking, but my answer is no" will suffice. You don't really owe anyone an explanation.

2. Let things go undone.

This is extremely hard for many firstborns. When you see something that needs to be done, you want to do it, and you want to do it right now. Let's say you've had a long day at your shop, and you walk in the door at home and see a spot or two on the carpet. You think, *I really need to shampoo this carpet.*

Then you notice where the dining room walls have been streaked and smudged by too many dirty little fingers, and you think, *I ought to paint the walls again.*

Then you walk into the garage and are overwhelmed by the disorganized clutter your husband was supposed to clean out months ago, and you think, *I'm going to have to get out here and do it myself.*

It seems everywhere you look, there is work—something that needs to be done. And you know you're the one who's going to have to do it.

If this sounds like you, why not give yourself a break? You just worked a full day. Does the carpet really need to be shampooed now? The dining room painted? The garage organized?

Firstborns spend the majority of their lives weighed under a long to-do list. Why not take yourself out from under that weight?

3. Don't play the game.

Some people in your workplace will just rub you the wrong way. That's a fact of life. But guess who usually bugs you the most? You guessed it: the person with the same birth order as you. After all, if you're both firstborns, you're vying for control of a situation (however small or large it is). So the two of you begin a game of one-upmanship. He says and does something that makes him feel superior to you. You say and do something that makes you feel superior to him. . . . And the game continues.

That's crazy. Why even go there? If you have to work with the person, learn to get along—or find a different job.

4. Wait twenty-four hours before volunteering.

If a hand goes up to volunteer for a task, whose hand do you think it is? Yours! You as a firstborn have a natural tendency to take on more responsibility than you should. A project that will require you to work long hours? *Sure, I'll take it.* Become the leader of the local Girl Scouts? *Why not?*

225

Volunteer to babysit the neighbor's two girls while she's at work—even though it's your one day off? *What's one more child in the house?*

The best thing a firstborn can do is to wait twenty-four hours before saying yes to anything. You get yourself in trouble when you commit yourself on the spot, then later look at your Day-Timer.

And if no one else volunteers, why should it become your job? The fact that no one else wants to volunteer doesn't mean you have to.

5. Stand up for yourself.

If your co-workers are content to let you do the majority of the work in the office, speak up and tell them that that isn't fair and you are no longer going to be doing their work for them. If you are handling four or five projects at once while your co-workers have only one or two, go to your boss and explain the situation. Ask for a more equitable distribution of the workload. (If your boss isn't open to such an arrangement, perhaps you'd better start looking for a new job.)

Remember, people will count on you to do everything once they know that you *will* do everything.

Your boss might even say something like, "Oh, give that job to Marti. She's a real go-getter, and she loves to keep busy." He may never dream you're annoyed and overloaded unless you tell him exactly how you feel. Not everyone is as analytical as you

> Remember, people will count on you to do everything once they know that you *will* do everything.

226

are. If your boss is a baby of the family, his mantra will be, "Don't worry, be happy"—until something really hits the fan.

6. Learn to accept others' standards.

If your colleague isn't doing his report the way you think it should be done, guess what? It isn't any of your business, so don't waste time or energy worrying about it. If he asks for your advice, that's one thing. But there's no reason for you to feel you must do his work for him. You are not the world's police officer. So let life go on, even if it doesn't meet your standards.

7. Take time to relax.

Spend your lunch hour away from your work, reading a book. If you work from an office, go to a park or library or coffee shop. If you work from home, retreat to a room where you're not faced with piles of work. In other words, give yourself a break in the midst of each day. And during that time, don't ask yourself, *What should I be doing today?* but rather, *What would I like to do today?*

8. Don't box yourself in.

Setting goals and keeping a list of things you want to do is a wonderful thing. But if your life is becoming controlled by those things, it's time to take some scissors to the list. If you have too many things on your schedule, there's no room for flexibility, spontaneity, or rest, is there? Make sure your lists are working for you—not the other way around.

How Do You Handle Setbacks?

It was Bill Veeck, the late owner of the Chicago White Sox, who first made this statement: "I do not think that winning is the most important thing. I think winning is the only thing."[7] His words have been picked up, repeated, and paraphrased time and again, most notably by the late great football coach Vince Lombardi.

Is that what you believe? Is winning the only thing?

"Of course not," you say immediately. "I know better than that. You can't always win."

Okay, you may say it on the surface, but do you *really* know it deep down inside, where it counts?

What's your reaction when you get into your car after a co-worker humiliates you in a game of racquetball? What about when the promotion you should get goes to someone else? What if you work day and night for two weeks on a job, and the boss decides it's not good enough to show the client, or he takes the credit himself? What if you've been organizing a community event, and nothing turns out the way you wanted it to? What then?

These are situations that most of us have faced at one time or another at work. Of course you get ticked off and frustrated. But if you're a perfectionistic firstborn, these things can drive you completely up and over the nearest wall.

No one likes to lose. But the important thing is how you deal with those kinds of situations. Ask yourself these questions:

Did you take on more than you could reasonably handle?

Were you held back by any fears?

Did you prepare properly for the job?

Was the fault really yours, or did anyone else share in it (for example, your boss, who didn't give you adequate time to prepare and now is blaming you)?

Are your skills really in that area, or not?

Firstborns can take on the world, so they tend to take on too much of it at once. The next time you're asked to do a job, consider:

Is it realistic for me to tackle this job given the time constraints and other things on my plate?

Do I feel comfortable doing this job? Is it in my interest and skill area?

Will I have the help and resources I need to do the job?

Based on the answers to those questions, you can make the best, most informed decision possible.

And if you fail at that task? Again, is it the end of the world? Not really, though it may seem so at the time. No one has ever done anything great without taking a risk, without sticking their neck out a little.

When you fail, cut yourself some slack. Your failure isn't permanent, it isn't a contagious social disease, and it doesn't mean your character is shot. That failure has to do with only one event; it's not an evaluation of you as a person.

Now that's something to think about.

My Way or the Highway?

Too many firstborns, because they are analytical, logical, and driven, don't do well in life in general because they don't use

229

the leadership qualities they have. They may be leaders, but their co-workers see them as cold fish, dictators, or autocrats. They even joke over coffee about the firstborn.

That's because many firstborns see their work and business relationships in the light of this attitude: "It's my way or the highway."

Sure, they naturally know what to do when presented with just about any problem. But just because firstborns do things a certain way doesn't mean it's the only way. Someone else might have another just-as-good idea (or perhaps even a better one), if given the chance to share it. A firstborn might be a genius and create an incredibly brilliant computer part, but he still needs people to market and sell that product, or he won't get anywhere.

Guess what? Those marketing and salespeople won't be firstborns. They'll be the kind of people who just barely got through college, since socializing was more their thing.

> Just because firstborns do things a certain way doesn't mean it's the only way.

Truth is, the world is made up of all kinds of people, and every birth order is needed.

Firstborns can be so highly competitive that they are oblivious to the basic needs of others (such as a pat on the back for a job well done). They see the world focusing on them and their accomplishments (after all, Mom and Dad did). They often have little regard for others as a result. They don't mean to be that way; they just are. They see people as pawns—good for moving around as they see fit. Like the college football coach who didn't take his assistant coaches with him when he got the big job in the NFL. Then, when he went back to college coaching, he didn't take any of the pro coaches with him. What was he saying by those actions? Basically, "Thanks, guys, but you mean diddly-squat to me. I was just using you to get to a better position. See ya."

There are a lot of people like that in the world—they're all about business, but also all about self. Do they command respect? Yes. Not because people like them but because people fear them. They're ruthless, they're intimidating, and they run over people. Their actions and words say, "You'd better stay out of my way, because I know what's best for this company. I'm making the decisions here. Yes, there's a board, but I control the board. I'm the one who's important. You're just a peon."

Am I talking just about big shots of huge companies here? No, you can find these powerful firstborns as the principals of high schools, managers at Walgreens, play directors of community theaters, music directors of churches, and even librarians and Little League coaches. People live in fear around them, with good reason—these powerful firstborns use people for their own purposes until they're sucked dry. Then they show their co-workers the door, and those poor people walk through it, wondering what happened.

But as long as the firstborn is making bucks and fulfilling his mission, he thinks everything is just fine. Sadly, he's the only one who's fooled. If only he knew how far a little attitude adjustment would take him . . .

Hold On to That Two Cents, Please

Firstborns naturally jump into conversations. With your natural leadership and superior organization skills, you can get from point A to point B much quicker than your later-born co-workers. When presented with a problem, you know what to do in a short amount of time. So why not share it?

And so you do. You summarize the whole plan while the other nine employees sit there, staring, with jaws hanging open.

By the time you're done, your co-workers are clearly not pleased. *Uh, I thought this was supposed to be a* group *brainstorm*, they're thinking. *You're such a know-it-all and brownnoser.*

Adding your two cents in so quickly certainly isn't helping your relationship with your co-workers. And it probably isn't helping your relationship with the VP, who is leading the meeting. (Frankly, he's annoyed he didn't think of the solution first, and he's hating being shown up by one of his employees.)

Of course, you have a solution, and most likely it's a good one. In fact, it may be the best one. But when you're a firstborn in a brainstorm session, it's good to sit back for a while, see what others contribute, and then fine-tune your own ideas so you can present them in a logical, pleasant, relaxed way. For example, "I've been thinking . . . well, I'm not sure, but this just might work. I liked what Jake and Joan said about such and such. What if we did that and also did this. . . . ?" This way you are acknowledging that you've heard what other co-workers have said, you like their ideas, and you have another thought to add.

If you're the boss, you might want to say first, "I appreciate all of you and your input on this. After listening to all of you, I'm wondering—and I could be wrong—that if we started with this facet to the company and then came around to what you suggested, Mary and Ellen, then . . ."

All of a sudden, you have your co-workers and employees eating out of your hand. All along you've known where you're going, but you're simply leading them in that direction as a group, instead of coming in with full guns blazing like a gangster boss.

Now *that* is a win-win situation for everyone. Not a competitive "I'll show you what I know" show. That's the kind of a response that will earn you the trust and loyalty of your co-workers—and often the chance for a promotion. You'll have shown yourself not only as a creative and efficient problem solver but as someone who is an honest and

> Others will be so charmed, they won't know what hit them. They'll want to try out your ideas.

fair negotiator and good at relating to people. You'll have used your firstborn strengths to your advantage. Others will be so charmed, they won't know what hit them. They'll want to try out your ideas. And if you're the boss, the employees will want to please you, because you've included them.

Part of being a leader as a firstborn is including other people first—taking time to listen to them—before you put in your two cents.

And who knows? Their ideas might even change what you say.

It's All about Relationships

When you're a leader (whether of a couple workers in a KinderCare, 25 people in the shop at a diesel corporation, or

412 people at a company), you have to mesh your personality with the people you work with. If you don't, you won't have good relationships, and you can bet your wallet that your business won't thrive. Because that's what good business is all about—relationships.

In this day and age, you can buy just about anything on the Internet, so why would you need a salesperson to sell you anything? Yet salespeople continue to earn a living by selling services door-to-door and to companies. Why? Because it's all about relationship. If you're in authority over others, you have to get good at seeing life through their eyes. That means seeing their point of view.

Give 'Em What They Want!

Let's say you were a real-estate salesperson in a desert area, and your client said to you, "I know most of the houses in Tucson, Arizona, don't have grass. They have colored gravel in their front yards. But I don't want to look at any houses that have a desertlike landscape. I want something that has traditional architecture and landscaping. Grass, flowers, and trees already there would be a bonus." What would you show your client?

Well, if you were the real-estate salesperson my wife called, you'd show her a house with a desertlike landscape.

"What?" you're saying. "That doesn't make any sense. She just said that *isn't* what she wanted."

Exactly. That is what she said, and he wasn't listening. And you know what that said to her? *This guy doesn't care what I want.*

So what did Sande do? She refused to return his phone calls. Enough said.

This is simple stuff. It's not rocket science. If a customer tells you what they want, give them what they want if it's within your power to do so.

Good relationships in the workplace and with your customers have everything to do with seeing things from a different point of view.

That's what successful firstborns learn how to do—and they do it well.

How to Treat Your Customers Right

As a firstborn, relationships are not usually your first priority. Getting the job done is. That's why you have to work especially hard at using your firstborn skills to your best advantage in relationships.

Bob Shaff, founder and president of Customers for Life Consulting (www.cflconsulting.com), is a firstborn who has done it right. He's an engaging, affable, compassionate, service-oriented, organized achiever and a hard worker. He has the smile, the personality, and the attitude that gathers people around him. That's because he knows a successful business is all about relationships. It's about having people on your team who are different from you and complement your skills. And it's about relating to customers in a way that makes them want to come back to you for future service.

Bob shared with me his "14 Actions Your Company Can Take to Earn

> Good relationships in the workplace and with your customers have everything to do with seeing things from a different point of view.

235

Customer Loyalty," and I loved the principles. They can be applied to every business. And with his permission (thanks, Bob), I now share them with you.

14 Actions Your Company Can Take to Earn Customer Loyalty

1. *Maintain a customer profile database.*

   Collect customer contact information. Use it to keep track of your customers and to stay in touch with them.

2. *Treat different customers differently.*

   Know (learn) who your best customers are. Start by treating them differently . . . specially.

3. *Interact with your customers.*

   Find innovative ways to have dialogue with your customers. Teach them about you. Ask them about their needs and preferences. Never talk *to* customers; talk *with* customers.

   Use meetings, telephone, fax, mail, newsletters, email, lunches, letters, invitations, thank-yous, updates, product announcements, new service announcements, and helpful hints as reasons to interact.

   Host customer meetings. Share your expertise with your customers. Put some fun in your business.

4. *Find ways to add value for your customers.*

   Ask your customers what they would like, and what they would prefer, and how they would like it: delivered, billed, guaranteed, serviced, and upgraded. Also ask your employees for ideas.

5. *Personalize everything you do for your customers.*

   Use their name. Show their account. Give them information the way they want it. Celebrate their businesses and anniversaries. Take and use their pictures. Give them credit. Publicize their use of your company.

6. *Say thank you.*

You can't say it too often; especially when you thank them for their business and their referrals.

Offer incentives for referrals. "Thank you" is to customer loyalty as "I love you" is to a marriage.

7. *Do unexpected things on unexpected times for your customers.*

To say thank you. To show you care. To show you value their business. To make them feel special. To add the "wow" factor to your business.

8. *Inject your company with regular, systematic collections of customer feedback.*

Every month, every quarter, ask customers, "How are we doing?" "What can we do better?" Share their answers with your employees.

9. *Welcome customer complaints.*

Make it easy to complain (and to praise). Act on their suggestions. Apologize, and give a little bit extra.

Let everyone know about what you are changing because of the suggestions.

10. *Sweat the "small stuff."*

Customers judge you on everything. Try to make 100 things 1 percent better. Identify and improve all your "Moments of Truth" (the ways your customers come in contact with your company).

11. *Hire the right employees, and train them in using customer service skills.*

Hire for attitude, train for skill. Provide the "tools" to fill customer needs and to handle customer complaints.

12. *Form a Customer Advisory Council of your best customers.*

    Meet quarterly to say thank you and to gather ideas on things you're doing, considering, or worried about.

13. *Create partnerships with related companies that can add value to your customers.*

    Use these partnerships to offer special "deals" to your customers.

14. *Reward your employees, who reward your customers, who reward your company, by doing business with you.*

    Employees are your most important and best customers. Treat them that way.[8]

Whether you work in an office or out of your home, these rules, adapted to your company, could turn your business around—and make you the talk of the town.

The Leader in You

If you're in authority over others—whether you're in charge of the volunteers for pizza day at your local school or for a political campaign, or you're a manager at McDonald's or a Fortune 500 company—you have to understand that you need to get good at seeing life through other people's eyes. That includes people who work for you and with you, as well as your customers.

For example, if you're working with someone who needs clear direction, then make the task that lies ahead of them clear. As time goes by, you'd be smart to check on how the person is doing. Most people won't react negatively to your finding out where they are with a project if you approach them as a valued member

> Hire for attitude (willingness and flexibility), because you can always teach skills.

of the team. They'll view your interest as, *He cares what I'm doing*, rather than, *Oh, no, he's checking on me.* The response of the people who work under you (whether volunteer, part-time, or full-time) has everything to do with the way you approach them.

Stephen Covey, the great business writer, says to start with the end in mind. So what do you want the outcome in your work to be? And how are you going to get there? You start by getting one person at a time in your court. Hire for attitude (willingness and flexibility), because you can always teach skills. As Bob Shaff told me, "There are things that a company can't train. A favorite quote of mine is, 'Never try to teach a pig to sing. It wastes your time and irritates the pig.' If you need a pig, hire a pig, but if you need a singer, don't hire a pig. If you need to provide great customer service, hire a happy, friendly, smart, innovative person and train them in the details of your business. Don't hire a person with ten years' experience in your business, who last smiled about five years ago."

How right you are, Bob.

So what do you, as a leader, need to do? Here are the principles that I live by and teach to businesspeople across the country:

239

1. Discover the SHAPE of your workers.

S = strength

H = heart

A = attitude

P = personality

E = experience

The people you choose to work with will either make your management easier or make it harder. If you end up with a healthy person, you'll be okay. If you don't, you'll end up with someone else's problems.

Don't ever take a letter of recommendation as the basis for hiring a person. Often people write great recommendation letters in the hopes that they'll find someone like you to hire the person and get her out of their hair.

2. Help your co-workers identify with you.

A CEO once told me, "The most important thing in business is that you have to let your people win. You don't take the credit for the great sales margin that your company was able to reach this quarter. You celebrate it with the worker bees who contributed to make it. You're always the last person to take a bow. You have to have integrity, and then your co-workers will want to be identified with you and with the company." As I always tell my kids, "Remember, you're a Leman." Worker bees also want—and need—to belong.

Oprah Winfrey has the corner on the market for this aspect of business, as far as I'm concerned. She has tremendous influence, uses humor, is a survivor of a difficult childhood, is a doer, loves people, and is an interesting conversationalist who makes you feel important. Now that's a leader. And people would knock down walls for her.

It all goes back to relationships. If you make a mistake and a customer gets angry and upset, but then you make good on it, that customer is going to tell at least twenty people a week about your marvelous company. There's gold in that.

High standards, honesty, and integrity never go out of style.

3. Treat everyone as important—because they are.

Every position has importance, from the janitor on up. As a guy who consulted in school systems for a number of years and taught teachers' in-services, I know that the smart teacher is the one who always has a great relationship with the custodian/janitor, who has keys for every place in the school. Employees need to know they are important—and appreciated.

Another thing to remember is that no one person is more important than the group.

Did you ever see the movie *Hoosiers*? In that movie, a basketball team from Indiana ends up winning the state championship in the 1950s. But it isn't easy. Coach Norman Dale, played by Gene Hackman, has to bench the star player because he's a hotshot and not a team player. There are the usual five players on the floor; then a guy fouls out. So what does the hotshot do? He starts pulling off his warm-up jersey to head back into the game.

"Where are you going?" the coach says.

Meanwhile, the referee comes over. "Coach, you only have four on the floor. You need five."

241

And you know what Norman Dale says? "My team is on the floor." And he tells the hotshot to sit down.

Now that's the sign of a healthy business—no one player is more important than the team. And that makes everyone feel safe and important.

4. Make your workplace a safe place to be.

Keep your employees well informed. Don't throw them curveballs or leave them hanging in the dark. Don't confuse boundaries with bridles. No one wants to be micromanaged. But they do want to be noticed and patted on the back for their work.

Are co-workers allowed a free expression of ideas, without threat of repercussions? If people have grievances, are they allowed to air them, or are they swept under the rug or punished? I worked for a company once that had a "godfather," a human resources specialist who could help employees with everything from money taken out of their paychecks to concerns about sexual harassment—someone we could talk to about anything.

Is there a rebel, an instigator who's causing trouble in the group? If so, you need to get rid of that person for the welfare of the group. Everyone needs to know that they are safe from emotional and physical harm at your company, and that no one is above the law. That will create an atmosphere of safety, growth, and respect among all employees.

5. Don't give problems time to fester.

If there's a problem between employees, get the two principals of the argument together and let them work it out. If they can't work it out, you can be the lightning rod that fosters clear direction, communication, and a resolution where everyone is basically happy. (Sometimes you won't be able to do this, but that is your goal.)

When one of your employees is in trouble or can't keep up, act quickly. Make a plan. Check in more frequently with that employee to see if he is meeting the day's goals. Don't leave him to flounder by himself, and don't just blow him off and hire someone else. People who like you will work hard for you and be conscientious—especially if you give them grace and rescue them from a bad situation.

If you need to correct an employee, do it gently behind closed doors, not in front of his peers. Remember that we all make mistakes.

6. Leave room for advancement.

Rotating your employees to different positions can be very encouraging so they don't have to do the same thing day in and day out. The smart employer finds ways to make the mundane not so mundane. I once worked with someone at Bantam Dell who had started as a file clerk and ended up as senior editor there.

If you don't leave room for advancement, you encourage failure.

7. Make sure your employees see you in the trenches.

The former CEO of Southwest Airlines, Herb Kelleher, took great pride in going on the airplanes and handing out peanuts with the flight attendants. His spirit of fun is still reflected on Southwest flights today.

Contrast that with this example. When I worked as a janitor in a hospital, a fellow janitor and I were walking down the hallway and noticed that workmen were laying carpet in the administrator's office. The other janitor said to me, "Well, there goes my raise." Obviously he saw that the administrator was taking good care of himself by getting the new carpet, and he translated that in his mind as, *There isn't going to be any money left over for me and my raise.*

In any company that is more than a few people, there's usually a huge division between the top dog and the worker bees. It's the smart leader who goes into the company kitchen and compliments the cooks on the homemade soup they made for lunch. Most likely those cooks will go home and tell their family, "Hey, guess what? The *president* came in today and talked to me. He patted me on the back and thanked me for the great effort."

> **Great Things to Say**
>
> "Could you possibly help me?"
> "I'm not sure that this is right, but here's what I think. . . ."
> "Let me share with you how I see that."
>
> **Great Things Not to Say**
>
> "Here's the plan."
> "Hey, bucko, listen up."
> "I'm talking here."

It's All in the Approach

Firstborns have the power to make people angry—or to make them feel included. And that power is all in a firstborn's words and actions. Gentle words will knock down tough walls and barriers. The right actions will open doors. So why not use your natural firstborn skills to do business the excellent way—the firstborn way?

Empower People

Use your firstborn advantage by thinking logically to your benefit—help solve the problem, yet give credit to others who deserve it. Recognize those who have contributed to your work. Give input to those who work with you. Gently point out what people do wrong, then give them another chance. That's what "empowering your employees"—a catchphrase of today's business world—is all about. That's when others truly see you as the leader you are. One of the best joys in life is coming alongside others and being happy for their success.

When businesses care about their employees, they look out for their welfare. That's why many businesses today have child care available at the place of employment. It's one of the ways they say, "Look, employee, we care about you. We understand your needs. And we want to help."

Surround Yourself with Other Birth Orders

Birds of a feather may flock together as friends, but they cause all sorts of trouble in the workplace. Surround yourself with people who balance you. If you want a focus group to look at a potential new product, and you had your choice of firstborns or babies of the family, which ones would you pick? I'd suggest the babies, because they're known for being more open to new ideas and to change.

But if the product flies, who will you need to organize the production? The firstborns. They're the fastest organizers and can see the whole picture.

What about the middleborns? They'll be the middle management—the negotiators who keep the peace between the firstborns, the babies, and the customers.

And the babies? They'll be your top salespeople.

It's a wonderful, grand circle, with everyone doing what they're best at.

Learn to Ask Rather Than Demand

When you simply say, "Could you possibly help me?" people can't turn you down. (Even the toughest person isn't going to say, "Go drop dead" in response to such a plea.) Even better, that person feels good that you think she's competent and up to the task you're asking of her. It's an invitation rather than a demand. And that's the best door opener.

Approach Criticism Quietly

If you grew up with a critical-eyed parent, you're more likely to be a criticizer (your employees would probably call you a pain in the old keister), and you'll create an atmosphere of fear and division. You'll spend your life micromanaging your co-workers, just as your parents micromanaged you. Why? Because that's the way you see life, and your legacy will continue.

If someone makes a mistake, you nail 'em. If they make another mistake, you get rid of 'em.

If someone is scheduling a project, you hover over them (like the gestapo parent who hovered over your schoolwork to make sure you got it done).

If someone shares a stupid idea, you fire back, "Where'd you get that idea from?" That puts the person in their place and makes them feel inferior.

But is that really smart? What have you gained in the long run?

What if you did this instead when an employee makes a mistake? Quietly come up and say to that employee, "I became aware of something yesterday, and I need to bring it to your attention. I found out you did such and such. Let's talk about that." Don't you think that would make a very different kind of impact?

Accept Criticism

If you're a pursuer of excellence, you're open to constructive criticism. You say, "Give me your best shot." You're not threatened by it. Your goal is to get the job finished in the most efficient manner. If your way isn't the best way to get the job done, you're open to suggestions.

Accepting criticism takes a lot of emotional maturity. But those who do it gain loyal co-workers.

Say Thank You

I believe in the power of the short note (compliments to Sande, who made me a believer). When others succeed, do something nice, or do something well, shoot 'em a note. It shows them they are appreciated, and it can lead to things you never dreamed.

Early in his career, my son, Kevin, was a page for Jay Leno. One time, when someone did something nice for him at the show, Kevin sent him a thank-you note. And since it's impossible for Kevin, who's an artist, to write a note without doodling something, he drew two NBC peacocks talking to each other about a third peacock. NBC had just celebrated its seventy-fifth anniversary, and the two peacocks were saying about the third, "If she's 75, she's had some work done."

The guy got the note and showed it to someone else, who showed it to someone else, who was a man of great influence.

Kevin's short note resulted in his being tucked under that person's wing. And that same person became a great adviser to Kevin as he launched his career from an entry-level position to a producer and comedy writer, with two Emmys to his credit, at the age of 29.

> Say thank you. Manners never go out of style.

What did Kevin do? He simply used his natural firstborn personality—his organized nature, determined follow-through, and combination of humor, artistic ability, and clever wording—to write the note.

You just never know what can happen.

So say thank you. Manners never go out of style.

Be Available

The CEO who gets out of his $5,000 leather chair, leaves his penthouse office, and comes and eats in the lunchroom with the regular workers is more likely to have a successful business. Why? Because that's what impresses people. That's something they will always remember. And everyone, as well as the work, benefits as a result.

The Heart of a Leader

The cost of being a firstborn leader is great. You're going to make tough decisions that aren't always popular, and sometimes people aren't going to like you. But are you known for your integrity? For your justice? For your heart?

Leaders who have big offices, make a lot of money, and want a lot of perks are a dime a dozen. But how many great leaders are there—leaders who admit they're not perfect?

True leaders are honest and humble. They admit they're not perfect. They remember who helped them get to where they are.

Remember the old Kenny Rogers song "She Believes in Me"? Who believes in you? How did you get to where you are now?

My friend Jerry Kindall was a member of the Minnesota Twins American League championship team. As a winner of the championship, he received a ring, anchored with a sizable diamond, that could choke a horse. After Jerry's pro career ended, he became the head baseball coach at the University of Arizona, where he won three national championships.

What do you suppose Jerry did with that huge ring?

I ran into Georgia, Jerry's wife, one day. She was wearing a gorgeous diamond pendant. "What a beautiful pendant," I said.

"Didn't I tell you about this?" she said.

"No." I shook my head.

"My Jerry gave it to me," Georgia said, smiling.

And I knew instinctively where that diamond had come from because I know the kind of man Jerry Kindall is.

When I talked to Jerry about it, I couldn't help but ask, "How could you do that?" I mean, he had won three national baseball championships at the college level. And he had won that big championship ring. How could he give that up?

"Oh, Kevin, it was one of the easiest things I ever did in my life. I was admiring my ring one day and realizing how much it meant to me. I decided right then and there that I had to share that ring with those I love the most."

So what did he do? He had a jeweler melt it down and make pins for his four kids, and he gave his wife a beautiful diamond pendant to hang around her neck. He had taken that ring of success and shared it with those he loved the most—those who had helped him get where he is.

Now there's the mark of a great leader—and yes, Jerry is a firstborn.

Great leadership isn't just professional; it's personal. If you treat those in the trenches with you as important and take them along with you, they'll be loyal to you until the cows come home. They won't be swayed, because they know your heart, and they'll follow you to the ends of the earth.

Great leadership is not a technique. It's not a course you master. It's all about having the heart of a leader. It's about caring about the people you serve and service. It's about honesty, integrity, and inspiring others to perform at their peak potential because you respect them and consider them important members of the team. It's about servicing your customers by helping them obtain the products they need instead of trying to sell them what they don't want, just to make a buck. It's about thinking about the good of the group.

The question you as a firstborn need to ask yourself every day is this: "Who is going to pay for my leadership?" The only person who should ever pay for your leadership is *you*. When you make a mistake, you need to pony up in front of your co-workers. "You know, I erred in my judgment there. We need to reconsider and go another direction."

> The only person who should ever pay for your leadership is *you*.

If you admit your failures, you gain a tremendous amount of allegiance and trust from your co-workers. It goes back to the old adage: "If you want to be a winner in life, you have to learn how to lose."

As hard as it is for firstborns to admit, losing is a part of life. But balanced firstborns will use failures as stepping-stones to victory. You'll learn from your experiences. And that's because you've learned to pursue excellence instead of striving for perfection.

You are a leader, no question about it. But what kind of a leader are you going to be?

10

The Firstborn Advantage in Relationships

Why birds of a feather flock together . . . but sometimes cause problems in the nest.

I t's funny how some memories stay with you all your life.
I'm not talking about those big events you'd be expected
to remember, like your graduation from high school or your
wedding day. I'm referring to those ordinary afternoons from
so many years ago that somehow stick in your mind.

Many of those memories for me have to do with my firstborn sister, Sally. And even at my age, the memories are as
clear and sharp as if the events happened yesterday.

I remember the parties we threw out in the backyard. She
and I were usually the only guests. She'd give me a quarter,
and I'd walk the half mile or so to the store, where I'd buy

two bottles of pop and a bag of pretzels. (Okay, so that was a *very* long time ago!)

When I got back, we'd set up our table, get our teacups, and celebrate nothing in particular—just being together, I suppose. Why do I remember those times? Because Sally was, is, and always will be an extremely important person in my life.

And that's the way it is with firstborns. You are often supremely important in the lives of your younger siblings (even if you don't think so). You may not realize how highly your siblings think of you.

They may be jealous at times. They may resent the fact that you get to stay up later and get a bigger allowance. They may do anything they can to annoy you and pester you. I sure did my share of annoying my firstborn sister. I remember waking her up one fine morning by dangling a big, juicy night crawler in front of her nose. But underneath all of my little-brother antics, I loved and respected my sister. I wanted to be just like her (even if she was a girl).

Now, looking back on those parties with Sally, I'm amazed. I'm still not sure why she was so willing to spend time with me or why she talked to me as a peer. She never treated me like a little kid or a pesky little brother (and I was both). She took me into her confidence and gave me some straight talk when I needed it (and I did). She made sure I was headed in the right direction.

I remember one of our early conversations. I think it went something like this:

"Do you like girls?" Sally asked me.

"Yuck. No way. Why would I like girls?" I was busy making a scooter and didn't even look up. I couldn't figure out why she was bothering me at a time like this. I had far more important things on my brain. Yes, sir, these old apple crates were going to be perfect for the body, but where was I going to find the right wheels? Hmm . . . maybe Sally's old pair of roller skates would work.

Then her voice interrupted my thoughts. "Do you like *me*?"

This seemed like the best time in the world to like her *very* much, especially when I thought about those skates.

"Of course I do."

"But I'm a girl."

My jaw dropped. Finally I mumbled, "That's different. You're my sister. And you're not like any of the other girls I know. . . . By the way, sis, remember those old skates—?"

"Well, I want to tell you a few things about girls."

I didn't really want to hear those few things, but Sally was going to tell me anyway (she did have a firstborn's determination, after all). She told me what girls were like, how they ought to be treated, and how I could go about getting a particular girl to like me.

At the time I thought the conversation was ridiculous. Why in the world would I care what girls liked? I was sure, as most 6- or 7-year-old boys are, that I'd grow up to be a confirmed bachelor—you know, just a man and his dog against the world.

Fast-forward six years. I suddenly discovered that girls weren't quite the blot on society that I'd always figured them to be. Then I remembered those talks with my sister. You know what? The information was quite useful.

It wasn't just in the area of girls that Sally helped me. I often needed her wisdom and advice (and her discipline). Sally sacrificed for me. When I was in kindergarten, she allowed me to sit on the seat of her bike while she walked me all the way to school, which had to have been a mile from the house. I always felt calm and assured when she was around, no matter what the situation was.

It's no wonder that I married a firstborn, when I got the sort of treatment I received from my firstborn sister. Perhaps it is because my sister and I were so different that we got along so well—and we still have a close relationship today.

Surprising Friendships

Think of your closest friends. Who are they, and how old are they in comparison to you?

Firstborns generally tend to get along better with people who are older or younger than they are. When you think about it, that makes sense. After all, you spent a lot of time by yourself in the adult world, bonding with your parents. And then if any siblings came along, you spent a lot of time taking care of them. So you're less familiar with peer friendships than you are with those of other ages.

Sometimes a firstborn will have several friends who are older and several who are younger, but not very many the same age. The age difference may be ten or fifteen years, or it may be two or three.

For example, my firstborn friend Rob says that none of his really good friends were in his class in high school. They were all a couple of years younger.

Linda's best friend in high school was her art teacher, who spent hours teaching her how to paint landscapes with pastels. "There was no one my age who was interested in art like I was," Linda says. "My best days were when I could go straight from school to Emily's art studio, and Emily would always have cookies and tea waiting for me. We'd always talk before we got started." Linda's other close friend was a rancher's wife who was in her thirties.

Eric's best friend growing up was an older gentleman named Tom who ran a fix-it shop in their small town. "At the time I thought he was really old," Eric says, laughing. "But he was only in his forties." Eric remembers stopping by after school every day to talk to Tom for a half hour before he went to his job at a department store. "I had a few friends my age, but there was no one I could talk to like Tom. We always had a lot to talk about, and it seemed more interesting than the stuff the other guys wanted to talk about. It just seemed we were on the same wavelength."

> **Who Are Your Friends?**
>
> List your closest friends—the friends you would call "heart friends."
> Are they older, younger, or your age?
> What do you share in common?

Rob, Linda, and Eric are fairly typical firstborns. They were more comfortable with people a little older or younger than themselves. Is there anything wrong with that? Of course not. Friendships can come in all ages and stages of life. A true friend is someone you're comfortable with and can share your heart with.

What friends play that role in your life?

Making Friends

Because firstborns often feel more comfortable around those who are older or younger, they often feel lonely in school or group situations where they are with others the same age.

When Sharon moved to town, she felt very lonely. She had just graduated from college and had a new job, but she couldn't seem to find a circle of friends. Most of her co-workers were recent college graduates too, but she just didn't connect with them. Everything they were interested in—Starbucks, shopping, jazz dancing—was not her thing. And they didn't really seem interested in doing anything with her. Frankly, they seemed unfriendly.

Sharon had no idea that because she was uncomfortable around others her age, she made *them* uncomfortable. Her uneasiness had been noticed by her co-workers. They all felt that Sharon was sending out a message for them to keep their distance, so they did.

It took several months, but Sharon finally met some women from her job's accounting division. Three of them were antique hunters, just like her. It wasn't long before the four women—Sharon (22), Eliza (37), Tamara (44), and Toni (53)—were regularly getting together on Saturdays for garage sales and antique marts. They even decided to go on a weekend trip to nearby Galena, Illinois, a town that had many antique stores. Sharon had finally found her friend group.

Quality versus Quantity

It's not unusual for firstborns to be able to count their good friends on one hand. Firstborns aren't likely to have a great many friends. That's why it sometimes bothers them when their middleborn or baby brothers or sisters have so many friends.

Sisters Reagan and Rachel, a firstborn and a baby, shared an apartment for the first three years after Rachel got out of college.

"If it wasn't the phone ringing, it was the doorbell, and it was always for her," Reagan says. "The noise drove me crazy. But what was worse is that no one ever called me or came to see me."

That's because it's much easier for laterborns to find friends. Middleborns have a lot of experience being in the middle, so they make friends easily. They have learned to be good negotiators, masters of compromise (keeping everyone happy), and the sort of people who can get along with almost anyone. (That's why having a middleborn in a marriage jacks up the probability of the marriage's success.)

Then there are the babies of the family, like Rachel, who are the charming entertainers and live for their social life.

"But it was interesting," Reagan says. "After a while I started to notice that none of her friends were the same. They seemed to change every month or two."

That's not unusual for laterborns either. They sometimes change friends as often as folks change underwear. I know of one girl who had dozens of friends, but they seemed to be on an ever-changing roster—she had three "very best friends" in six months' time.

When firstborns establish relationships, they are usually more lasting and loyal. Isn't one lasting relationship worth more than a dozen that come and go?

Birds of a Feather?

The old adage that birds of a feather flock together is certainly true when it comes to friends. You do tend to flock with people of your own birth order when it comes to friendships. That's why groups like the First Born Girls Social Club are so successful.

However, firstborn males are not likely to have very many meaningful relationships. In fact, if a male has one guy he can really talk to, he's blessed. To most firstborn males, communicating is like a grunt over the punch bowl at a party. That grunt is a whole conversation:

"Hi."

"Hi."

"Nice party we're havin."

"Yeah."

"How 'bout those Chicago Bears?"

"Yeah. Good game."

And then both firstborns move off, satisfied that they've had a conversation; neither requires more interaction.

If the firstborn is more extroverted, he may have a few more friends. But when it gets right down to it, are they really friends, or just co-workers and acquaintances? Does the firstborn share his heart, or just information? Is talking just a means to an end? And is he satisfied with those relationships? Most men would say yes—and then move on to the next thing on their brains, like the football game or surfing the Net.

That's why, for firstborn males, having one person in their life they can talk to—oftentimes a spouse—is enough, and they're satisfied with that.

With women, the ante is upped in relationships because women—even firstborns—talk, share, and communicate by their very nature. They talk for connection—and, let's face it, they talk for entertainment. That's why relationships— finding friends who will share their heart—are extremely important for all women. And where do women go to find friends? To places where they might find women just like them.

So where can you as a firstborn go to meet people?

Do you like math? Then you might find a soul mate at the math club—someone who wants to be a future engineer, just like you do. And I bet you anything that the people there will arrive on time for the club. Most likely, they're all firstborns too.

Do you enjoy making clay pots? Why not volunteer at a local farm to give pottery-making demonstrations?

Do you like to play tennis? Try the Saturday morning club.

Because firstborns see life as so clear and crisp—in terms of black and white, right and wrong—they will tend to flock to others who like the same things and have the same perspective.

Having friends who are just like you can be fun . . . for a while. But if you're a critical-eyed firstborn, chances are you have a critical-eyed person among your group of friends.

Let's see if I'm right. Take a look at the list of friends you jotted down from page 257. Star the names of any friends who tend to be critical.

Are they the same people who tend to irritate you? Why do you think that is? Maybe because they're good at pointing out your flaws? "You know, Miriam, that swimsuit isn't very flattering." "You could have more patience, you know. . . . Why are you so grouchy today?"

If there's one thing you don't need as a firstborn, it's someone who points out your flaws. You do enough of that on your own.

261

Are You Sabotaging Yourself?

When you as a firstborn try to make friends, you have all the best intentions. But what you don't realize is that you sometimes sabotage your own efforts. Don't let these areas keep you from enjoying a variety of friendships.

Are You Too Opinionated?

Firstborns tend to be opinionated. You have strong stances on everything from religion to politics, and you usually make your views known. But what makes the world go 'round is discussion—a give-and-take that makes both parties feel important and knowledgeable. Just because they're your ideas doesn't mean those ideas are the only way to fly.

Instead, you need to make sure you allow your friends time to speak freely and share their ideas. Yours aren't the only ideas that count. Asking your friends what they think about a situation and how they think you should handle it invites relationships. Firstborns, you see, are great at telling people what to do but not great at inviting relationships. That's why you're often called bossy.

> If there's one thing you don't need as a firstborn, it's someone who points out your flaws. You do enough of that on your own.

What Drives a Firstborn Up the Wall

A late lunch date (who doesn't have any excuse that can hold water)
A friend who can't find her Day-Timer to make an appointment
Mismatched socks
The color gray

Do You Jump In to Solve a Problem?

Firstborns tend to jump in to solve a problem. You're so quick to analyze a situation that you're miles ahead of everyone else. So if you've already figured out the answer, why not tell the world?

But do you want others to solve all your problems for you? Or do you sometimes just want to be heard and then figure out the answer on your own?

It's like playing poker. Let's say you're dealt four aces. What do you do? Do you throw your hands up in the air, yell "Woo-hoo!" and put a huge bet down? If you do, you'll probably scare everyone out of the game, and you sure wouldn't have much of a reward. But if you just play out the game, you'll win. No one else needs to know you hold all the high cards. You're just one of the players sitting around the table.

Sure, you may have the answer to a problem in your back pocket, but sometimes it's better to let someone else go first, to include other people in the "game" instead of playing it all by yourself.

Are You a Know-It-All?

Her name was Mandy. She was brighter than bright, but I wanted to pound her. You see, back in the days when I struggled through Latin class, she was one of those brown-nosing little suckers who sat up close to the teacher's desk. I was there only because the teacher was determined to keep an eye on me. It was one of the best seats in the house, and I got it because I was a "behavior problem."

I can still see that Latin teacher calling on Mandy. Every time, it made me mad. I would have loved just three minutes alone with her. . . .

The point is, just because you have all the answers doesn't mean you always have to broadcast it.

This is especially important for the firstborn male to know. Men, if you spout off the answer to a woman's question, she will probably be turned off. When a woman poses a question to you, she's not asking you to fix anything; she just needs you to know what's up. Once you have all the information, wait, be patient, and see what she comes up with herself. (If men could do that, many relationship problems just might be solved—from the male side of the equation, that is.)

Do You Make All the Decisions?

Do you find yourself in the role of making all the decisions in the friendship? "Let's go see a movie on Friday night. I researched it, and here's the selection I like best." Or, "Listen, this is a slam dunk. Here's what we're going to do."

Do you want a friendship, or do you just want a yes person who agrees to whatever you want to do? By making all the decisions in the friendship, you're shutting off your friend's participation.

Do You Analyze and Overanalyze Everything?

You're so analytical that you can't seem to help it. You're always thinking about how to improve something, and that includes your friendships. But what if your friend doesn't want to improve the friendship in the same way? Firstborns can be so intense that laterborns back off.

The same skills that work well for you in the workplace and get you bonuses and promotions—being analytical, being organized, and going for the goal—are the same skills that can work against you in relationships.

Are You Perfectionistic and Critical?

Firstborns are always wishing for more—that the relationship could be something it's not. You're often critical of your friends and their decisions, especially if they hold a different view. (This is especially true since firstborns are black-and-white thinkers.)

Use Your Firstborn Advantage!

But here's the good news. Firstborns, more than any other birth order, are capable of change—and quick change. Because you are analytical, determined, and focused and you see issues so clearly, you can understand what changes need to be made in your relationship. You can use what you've learned to your own and your friends' advantage.

Be a Balanced and Gentle Leader in Your Friendship

Instead of jumping in with your opinion, ask the question, "What do you think about that issue?" Then sit back and listen to what your friend is *really* saying, rather than warming up all sides of your own response so you can be ready to fire. What you hear just might change your own opinion. You never know.

Let Your Friend Find a Solution for Herself

Remember that sometimes people talk because they are processing a situation and trying to find a solution themselves. Let

265

your friend do the talking. Perhaps she can resolve the problem on her own just by processing it with you. And if she comes to a different conclusion than you, so what? It is, after all, her problem, her solution, and her life. You don't always have to agree.

Refrain from Being a Know-It-All

No one likes a know-it-all. You don't either. Sometimes the smartest thing you can do is shut your mouth and listen to what others have to say.

Allow Your Friend an Equal Partnership

Why not trade off deciding what to do or where to go on your outings? Allow her equal talk time. The focus shouldn't be solely on you, your achievements, and your life. Your friend should have a 50 percent share in the deal. Sure, sometimes you'll talk more about her, and sometimes you'll talk more about yourself, but overall there needs to be an even split. Friendship should be an even exchange.

Put Your Analytical Skills to Work in a Different Way

Instead of trying to think how you could improve your friend, ask, "How can *I* become a better friend? What could I do to reach out to others who are like me, or unlike me? In what way(s) am I inviting friendships? In what ways am I scaring people off?"

Lighten Up

It isn't the end of the world if your friend wears a bad bathing suit, if she can't get together when you want to because she has to study for her night class, or if she doesn't understand the intricacies of the galaxy like you do.

It takes all kinds to make the world go 'round.

> It takes all kinds to make the world go 'round.

A Marriage Made in Heaven?

Since we're talking about relationships here, I'd be remiss if I didn't mention finding that special person. Since firstborns are so focused, it can be a challenge to befriend those of other birth orders because, well, they're so different. But aren't relationships, after all, about compromise?

Yes, it's true that in friendships you tend to flock together with those of the same birth order. But the best marriages are the exact opposite. Birds of a feather may flock together, but they'd better think twice before they build a little nest for two. There's no clash as great as when two perfectionistic firstborns or, worse, two only children get married. The result can be pure disaster.

Am I saying that love can't conquer all? No. But if you're a firstborn or an only child who's planning to marry another firstborn or only child, you'd better make sure you have a tremendous amount of love in your heart.

Firstborns tend to be strong willed, to be sure of themselves, and to have strong points of view. Put two of them together in a marriage relationship, and you're likely to find out what happens when an immovable object tangles with an unstoppable force—a lot of heat, noise, and confusion. And usually it's over little things like where the toothpaste tube is squeezed, where the sprinkler goes on the lawn, who is leaving a mess, etc.

Can two firstborns be happily married to each other? Certainly. I've seen it countless times with firstborns who had a clear division of labor (who is going to do what) in their relationship. But no marriage between two firstborns will be successful without a lot of compromise, without admitting perfectionistic tendencies, and without agreeing to yield to one another.

> Birds of a feather may flock together, but they'd better think twice before they build a little nest for two.

Generally, a marriage involving two people from the same birth order, whatever that birth order may be, is not good. That's because both of them are weak in the same areas, and they will drag each other down in those areas. I hate to think what my marriage would be like if I were married to another fun-loving and spontaneous lastborn. We'd never get anything done.

So who is the ideal marriage partner for a firstborn? It has to be the lastborn. I'm not just saying that because of all the years I've been married to Sande and the wonderful relationship we've had. I'm saying it because the first-and-last combination works so well. The strengths and weaknesses of the husband and wife tend to complement each other.

The fun-loving lastborn can teach the firstborn to relax and take things a little less seriously. The firstborn can keep the lastborn anchored so he doesn't go floating off into space. The lastborn can temper his mate's tendencies toward perfectionism. The firstborn can help her spouse understand that sometimes life does need to be taken seriously.

If there's anything that could be considered a marriage made in heaven, it's probably a marriage between a firstborn and a lastborn.

Something Old, Something New . . .

Think for a minute about an artist's color palette. Let's say you add blue and blue. What do you get? Blue. Plain blue.

But if you blend blue and green, what do you get? Teal.

You see, it's the blending of the two colors that makes something new and beautiful.

And that's exactly what happens when you find lasting relationships. They bring a new color to your life.

11

Making the Most
of Being a Firstborn

What do you really want out of life? You can break
free of your own and others' expectations.

Okay, the contest is over. You win. No one is challenging
your supremacy or the wonderful things you do.

As a firstborn, you've been given great gifts. You're the
organizer, the visionary, the doer, the planner. Your parents
taught you discipline and respect. You're not a slacker. You're
the person others look up to—the leader. You have the answers; you're ahead of the rest of the pack.

Let's review your top character traits as a firstborn.

You're a Natural Leader

The world needs people like you who have the courage and
the willingness to lead. So give yourself a chance, and others

will see your leadership abilities. When you were a child, your younger siblings looked to you as their leader. Once you've assumed the mantle of leadership, it's not easy to take it off. But oh, the things you can do. Look ahead with great anticipation!

You're a Great Analyzer

You're noted for asking a great many questions and for wanting to know all the details. Sometimes you can drive less-patient types just a little bit crazy.

But you shouldn't apologize for your questioning nature. There's nothing wrong with wanting to know all the details so you can have a firm handle on a situation. It's all part of your firstborn nature. Once you understand the situation, you can figure out a step-by-step procedure for doing what must be done.

If it weren't for meticulous firstborns, some of the rest of us might go on running around in circles forever.

I've never had any patience with a Rubik's Cube. When I'm challenged to try one, I give it a few minutes and then, when I can't get the solution, I'm through with it. It's my baby-of-the-family nature to be impulsive and impatient with technical, logical, analytical things. But I've seen others spend huge amounts of time with one of those cubes— studying it, analyzing it, working on it with seemingly infinite patience. What's the difference? I'd be willing to wager that those who worked so hard at solving that puzzle were firstborns.

That analytical, thought-out approach is what serves you so well in many areas. So why not learn to apply your natural, everyday thought processes to your best advantage? Don't let the rest of us—the impatient, impulsive ones standing in line behind you—push you to a hasty and poorly thought-out decision.

You're the type of person who, if presented with a job offer, makes two columns for the pros and cons on a piece of paper. Then you write down everything you can think of in those columns and really scrutinize the situation. Although others may be impatient with that, keep in mind that no one ever messed up their life by thinking too carefully about a decision.

> No one ever messed up their life by thinking too carefully about a decision.

You're a Scholar

You're always thinking, always learning. You devour books and magazines. This too gives you a head start on the world.

Mom and Dad bought you lots of books—such as *The Little Engine That Could, Babar Comes to America,* and *Green Eggs and Ham*—and then read to you at bedtime every night. All this reading developed in you a love for books and an appreciation for reading.

Then your brother came along and your parents no longer had time for those reading sessions. But you began reading a few simple books on your own. By the time you went to kindergarten, you had a jump on your education and were ahead of other children in the classroom.

It's no wonder so many firstborns are teachers, professors, and scientists and are involved in other professions that require serious scholarship.

Don't second-guess yourself. You don't always have to answer every question, but you don't have to play dumb to be accepted either. Just be who you are. Intelligent people will seek out intelligent people.

> You don't always have to answer every question, but you don't have to play dumb to be accepted either. Just be who you are.

You're the Master of Organization

When you were young, you must have heard your mom say, "A place for everything and everything in its place." She must have said it quite often, in fact, because you believe it with a passion.

Some of us laterborns might poke fun at the organized firstborn from time to time, but that's only because we're jealous of you. We spend hours every week hunting for something we know we put "right here," but it's gone. Later on, of course, we'll find it somewhere else, and then we'll realize that that was where we had really left it.

The organized firstborn wouldn't dream of doing that. It's not in your nature. It doesn't mean you don't have an occasional memory lapse, but your overall track record is much higher than middleborns or lastborns.

Being organized is not a curse; it's a blessing.

You're better at handling the family finances. You're better at planning the itinerary for the family vacation. Organization for you seems to be effortless. You make wonderful attorneys, journalists, accountants, and librarians. You do well in show biz, where you can combine organizational and creative skills. Firstborns Steven Spielberg and George Lucas are great examples.

Your desk may be a mess, but underneath it all, you know where everything is. You're a marvel at organizing.

You're structured, and you need your life to be that way. You need your to-do list. And what's wrong with that? Look at all the things you get done.

You're a Self-Starter

You're always a step ahead of the game. You have the ability to see what needs to be done and to get started on it. You're self-motivated and self-reliant, so you don't need much (if any) supervision.

One downside is that you may tend to do everything by yourself; it's not easy for you to delegate authority or responsibility. One of the criticisms of firstborn president Jimmy Carter was that he worked himself into exhaustion because he wouldn't delegate. If you can learn how to delegate, you'll be able to accomplish even more. Does that mean the job will always get done perfectly—as you would do it? No, but is that so bad, especially since it would be impossible for you, as a human being, to be everywhere at once?

The most important thing for you to remember is that you can't do it all. You have to delegate, and you have to work on your ability to say no. You can't handle everything, and you can't do whatever anyone asks you to. You must know your limits and then stick to them.

As a firstborn, you need to consciously take smaller bites of life. Otherwise you'll get yourself so involved in projects that you don't have any time left for yourself or your family.

If your skills are harnessed, you'll not only achieve your maximum potential, but you'll make a significant contribution to the world around you. To do that, you need to get behind other people's eyes and see the world as they see it. As a successful firstborn CEO friend of mine said, "Kevin, you have to let people win. It's not about you. It's about others, and how you can learn to be joyful for others as they succeed in life."

The words you say to your spouse, your children, and your co-workers can harm or heal. They can cut both ways—as helpful or hurtful. Encouraging or degrading. Uplifting or depressing. Those words will leave an indelible imprint.

That's a lot of power! And that power is a little like nuclear energy—if it's not maintained carefully and harnessed and dealt with delicately, it can blow up and cause tremendous damage for you and everyone around you.

You can be tremendously successful in your career but fail miserably in your relationships because you're not balanced. And you will pay the price for that (as will others).

Take firstborn Bill Clinton, a Rhodes Scholar, for instance. He was a successful, two-time president—charismatic, inspirational, well liked, on top of his game—but he wasn't in balance, and his lack of moral integrity became not just public but top news.

Yes, firstborn, you are the top dog, but you have to understand that you have a few fleas. Throughout this book, I've shown you how to take advantage of your firstborn skills so you can succeed in life. If you have grown up with a critical parent and, as a result, have struggled with procrastination and self-doubt, I have a couple books you should read: *When Your Best Isn't Good Enough* and *Pleasers*.[1] Those two books will give you even more insight into what makes you tick and why you act the way you do.

Your special strengths as a firstborn can be used to your best advantage. So why not:

take advantage of your birth order

overcome the perfectionism that holds you back

learn how to bounce back when you fail

find balance in your work and relationships

stick to your guns

find out what you really want out of life

say NO

develop meaningful relationships, with a healthy give-and-take

make choices because you want to, not because you have to

feel better about yourself

find some time for yourself

Success is waiting for you.

Notes

Introduction: Will the Firstborn Please Stand Up?

1. See Kevin Leman, "Appendix A: U.S. Presidents and Their Birth Order," in *The Birth Order Book: Why You Are the Way You Are* (Grand Rapids: Revell, 1998).

2. For more information, see "Appendix B: A Review of *Born to Rebel* by Frank Sulloway," in Leman, *The Birth Order Book.*

3. Laura Carter (founder, First Born Girls Social Club), in discussion with the author, October 26, 2007.

Chapter 1: What's This Birth Order Business About Anyway?

1. Alfred Adler, quoted in Bruce Bohle, *The Home Book of American Quotations* (New York: Dodd, Mead, and Co., 1967), 386.

2. See Jeffrey Kluger, "The Power of Birth Order," *Time*, October 17, 2007, http://www.time.com/time/health/article/0,8599,1672715,00.html.

3. Ibid.

Chapter 2: Who's on First?

1. Scott Fornek, "Half Siblings: A Complicated Family," *Chicago Sun Times*, September 9, 2007, http://www.suntimes.com/news/politics/obama/familytree/545462,BSX-News-wotrees09.stng.

2. Harold Bloomfield, *Making Peace in Your Stepfamily* (New York: Hyperion, 1993), 43.

3. Kevin Leman, *Living in a Stepfamily without Getting Stepped On* (Nashville: Thomas Nelson, 2001).

4. Karl Konig, quoted in Carol Hyatt and Linda Gottlieb, *When Smart People Fail* (New York: Simon and Schuster, 1987), 232–36.

Chapter 3: The Firstborn Personality

1. Carter, discussion.

2. Ibid.

Chapter 4: Why Firstborns Are the Way They Are

1. Taken from Laura Carter's invitation to the initial First Born Girls friends, November 2005. © by Laura Carter. Used by permission.

2. Joseph Price, "Birth Order Study: It's About Time," BYU News Release, Brigham Young University, http://byunews.byu.edu/archive08-feb-birthorder.aspx.

3. Leonardo da Vinci, quoted in Jane Goodsell, *Not a Good Word About Anybody* (New York: Ballantine Books, 1988), 50.

4. Miriam Adderholdt-Elliott, *Perfectionism: What's Bad About Being Too Good?* (Minneapolis: Free Spirit Publishing, 1987), 18–20. Concepts adapted.

Chapter 5: Where Do I Go to Buy One of Those Firstborns?

1. Carter, discussion.

2. First Born Girls Social Club Newsletter, November 2005. © Laura Carter. Used by permission.

3. Carter, discussion.

4. Ibid.

5. See www.firstborngirls.com for further information.

6. Carter, discussion.

7. Ibid.

8. Ibid.

9. Ibid.

10. Ibid.

Chapter 6: Has the Critical Eye Turned on You?

1. Kevin Leman, *What Your Childhood Memories Say About You* (Wheaton: Tyndale, 2007).

2. John Culhane, "Gene Hackman's Winning Wave," *Reader's Digest*, September 1993, 88–89.

3. Gene Hackman, quoted in Ellen Hawkes, "The Day His Father Drove Away," *Parade*, February 26, 1989, 10–12.

4. Nathaniel Branden, *How to Raise Your Self-Esteem* (New York: Bantam Books, 1987), 22–23.

Chapter 7: The Firstborn Advantage at Home

1. For more detailed information on this, read chapter 12 of Leman, *The Birth Order Book.* If you're a pleaser, I have a great book for you too: Kevin Leman, *Pleasers* (Grand Rapids: Revell, 2006).

2. Kevin Leman, *Be Your Own Shrink* (Grand Rapids: Revell, 2006).

3. Guess the Birth Order

When the phone rings in your home, who is it usually for? Lastborn
Your son is very concerned about a crease in his blue shirt. Who is he? Firstborn
"I just can't do it right now. I have to prepare first." Firstborn (can also be middleborn, depending on whether a critical-eyed parent is involved)

4. Match the Person to the Birth Order

Most likely to be stubborn:	firstborn
Most likely to be bossy:	firstborn
The negotiator:	middle child
Most likely to have a pet name:	baby
Most likely to point the finger of blame:	baby
Has the most friends:	middle child or baby
Most likely to say, "I don't care," when they really do care:	middle child
Could charm the socks off an elephant:	baby
Least likely to tell you how they feel:	middle child
Most secretive:	middle child
Most likely to show off:	baby

Chapter 8: The Firstborn Advantage at School

1. Benedict Carey, "Research Finds Firstborns Gain the Higher I.Q.," *New York Times*, June 22, 2007, http://www.nytimes.com/2007/06/22/science/22sibling.html?_r=1&st=cse&sq=Research+Finds+Firstborns+Gain+the+Higher+I.Q.&scp=1&oref=slogin.

2. Ibid.

3. Ibid.

4. "1986: Seven Dead in Space Shuttle Disaster," BBC, January 28, 2008, http://news.bbc.co.uk/onthisday/hi/dates/stories/january/28/newsid_2506000/2506161.stm.

5. *Meet the Press* with Tim Russert, October 21, 2007, http://www.christonium.com/politicalmusings/ItemID=11929826957353.

6. Adderholdt-Elliott, *Perfectionism*, 16.

7. Goodsell, *Not a Good Word*, 21.

Chapter 9: The Firstborn Advantage at Work

1. "Firstborn Children Often Grow into CEOs," *USA Today*, September 4, 2007.
2. Carey, "Research Finds Firstborns Gain the Higher I.Q."
3. Leman, *The Birth Order Book*, 352.
4. Ibid., 354–55.
5. "Firstborn Children Often Grow into CEOs."
6. Match the Occupation to the Birth Order

Anesthesiologist:	firstborn
Super salesman (could sell dead rats for a living):	lastborn
Comedian:	lastborn
Pharmacist:	firstborn
Social worker:	middleborn
Interior designer:	firstborn
Architect:	firstborn
Math teacher:	firstborn
Watchmaker/jeweler:	firstborn
English teacher:	firstborn
General sales manager:	firstborn
Manager:	middleborn
P.E. teacher:	lastborn
CEO:	firstborn
Diplomat:	middleborn
Electrician:	firstborn
Recreational therapist:	lastborn
Nurse:	firstborn
Attorney:	firstborn
Social studies teacher:	middleborn

7. Bill Veeck, Brainy Quote, 2008, http://www.brainyquote.com/quotes/quotes/b/billveeck173996.html.
8. "14 Actions Your Company Can Take to Earn Customer Loyalty," by Bob Shaff, © 2007 Customers for Life Consulting. All rights reserved. See http://www.cflconsulting.com for further information.

Chapter 11: Making the Most of Being a Firstborn

1. Kevin Leman, *When Your Best Isn't Good Enough* (Grand Rapids: Revell, 2007); *Pleasers* (Grand Rapids: Revell, 2006).

About Dr. Kevin Leman

An internationally known psychologist, radio and television personality, and speaker, Dr. Kevin Leman has taught and entertained audiences worldwide with his wit and commonsense psychology.

The bestselling and award-winning author has made hundreds of house calls for radio and television programs, including *The View* with Barbara Walters, *Today*, *Oprah*, CBS's *The Early Show*, *Live with Regis Philbin*, CNN's *American Morning*, and *Life Today* with James Robison. Dr. Leman has served as a contributing family psychologist to *Good Morning America*.

Dr. Leman is also the founder and president of Couples of Promise, an organization designed and committed to helping couples remain happily married. He is a founding faculty member of iQuestions.com.

Dr. Leman's professional affiliations include the American Psychological Association, the American Federation of Television and Radio Artists, the National Register of Health

Services Providers in Psychology, and the North American Society of Adlerian Psychology.

In 1993, he was the recipient of the Distinguished Alumnus Award of North Park University in Chicago. In 2003, he received from the University of Arizona the highest award that a university can extend to its own: the Alumni Achievement Award.

Dr. Leman attended North Park University. He received his bachelor's degree in psychology from the University of Arizona, where he later earned his master's and doctorate degrees. Originally from Williamsville, New York, he and his wife, Sande, live in Tucson, Arizona. They have five children.

For information regarding speaking availability, business consultations, or seminars, please contact:

Dr. Kevin Leman
P.O. Box 35370
Tucson, AZ 85740
Phone: (520) 797-3830
Fax: (520) 797-3809
www.lemanbooksandvideos.com

Resources by Dr. Kevin Leman

Books for Adults

The Birth Order Book
Sheet Music
Making Children Mind without Losing Yours
Sex Begins in the Kitchen
7 Things He'll Never Tell You . . . But You Need to Know
What Your Childhood Memories Say about You
Running the Rapids
What a Difference a Daddy Makes
The Way of the Shepherd (written with William Pentak)
Home Court Advantage
Becoming the Parent God Wants You to Be
Becoming a Couple of Promise
A Chicken's Guide to Talking Turkey with Your Kids about Sex (written with Kathy Flores Bell)
First-Time Mom
Keeping Your Family Strong in a World Gone Wrong
Step-parenting 101
The Perfect Match

Be Your Own Shrink
Say Good-bye to Stress
Single Parenting That Works
When Your Best Isn't Good Enough
Pleasers
Have a New Kid by Friday

Books for Children, with Kevin Leman II

My Firstborn, There's No One Like You
My Middle Child, There's No One Like You
My Youngest, There's No One Like You
My Only Child, There's No One Like You
My Adopted Child, There's No One Like You
My Grandchild, There's No One Like You

DVD/Video Series

Making Children Mind without Losing Yours (Christian—parenting edition)
Making Children Mind without Losing Yours (Mainstream—public school teacher edition)
Value-Packed Parenting
Making the Most of Marriage
Running the Rapids
Single Parenting That Works
Bringing Peace and Harmony to the Blended Family

Available at 1-800-770-3830 or www.lemanbooksandvideos.com

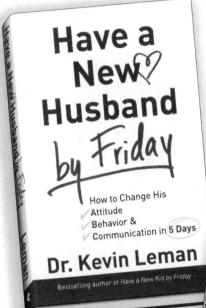
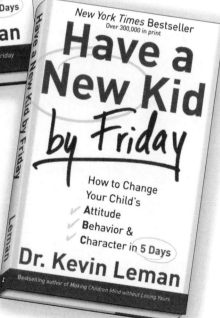

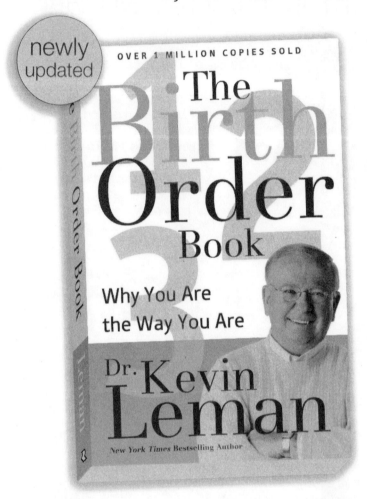